*The Crown
Crime Companion*

THE CROWN CRIME COMPANION

The Top 100
Mystery Novels of All Time

———————— ✦ ————————

Selected by the Mystery Writers of America

ANNOTATED BY OTTO PENZLER

COMPILED BY MICKEY FRIEDMAN

CROWN TRADE PAPERBACKS
NEW YORK

This volume is dedicated to the members of the Mystery Writers of America whose works fill these pages.

Copyright © 1995 by Mystery Writers of America, Inc.

Published by Crown Publishers, Inc., 201 East 50th Street, New York, New York 10022. Member of the Crown Publishing Group.

Random House, Inc. New York, Toronto, London, Sydney, Auckland

Crown Trade Paperbacks and colophon are trademarks of Crown Publishers, Inc.

Manufactured in U.S.A.

Book design by Deborah Kerner

Library of Congress Cataloging-in-Publication Data

The Crown crime companion : the top 100 mystery novels of all time / selected by the Mystery Writers of America : annotated by Otto Penzler ; compiled by Mickey Friedman.
    p. cm.
  1. Detective and mystery stories, English—Stories, plots, etc.
  2. Detective and mystery stories, American—Stories, plots, etc.
  3. Bibliography—Best books—Detective and mystery stories.
  I. Penzler, Otto. II. Friedman, Mickey. III. Mystery Writers of America.
PR830.D4C755   1995
016.823′087208—dc20
94-43825
CIP

ISBN 0-517-88115-2
10 9 8 7 6 5 4 3 2 1
First Edition

Contents

Acknowledgments   7

Introduction by Peter Ginna and Jane Cavolina   9

Making the Lists: A Saga by Mickey Friedman   11

Part One
THE LISTS

The Top 100 Mystery Novels of All Time
   Selected by Active MWA Members   17

Favorite Female Writer   81

Favorite Male Writer   81

Favorite Female Sleuth   81

Favorite Male Sleuth   81

Favorite Cities for Murder   81

Favorite Murder Weapon   82

Favorite Hiding Place for a Body   82

Favorite Animal in a Mystery Novel   82

Favorite Mystery Movie   82

Part Two
THE TOP TEN BOOKS BY CATEGORY

Classics by H. R. F. Keating   85

Suspense by Mary Higgins Clark   91

Hard-Boiled/Private Eye by Sue Grafton   97

Police Procedural by Joseph Wambaugh   103

Espionage/Thriller by John Gardner   109

Criminal by Richard Condon   115

Cozy/Traditional by Margaret Maron   121

Historical by Peter Lovesey   125

Humorous by Gregory Mcdonald   133

Legal/Courtroom by Scott Turow   139

Part Three

THE EDGAR WINNERS

Grand Master   145

Best Novel   145

Best First Novel by an American Author   154

Best Original Paperback   162

Best Fact Crime   167

Best Critical/Biographical Work   177

List of Contributors   182

Acknowledgments

We are grateful to Susan Moody and the British Crime Writers' Association whose *Hatchards Crime Companion,* published in England, was the inspiration for this book. Invaluable contributions to this project were made by Otto Penzler, whose wide-ranging knowledge of the mystery field made him the perfect choice to annotate the selections; Priscilla Ridgway, executive director of the Mystery Writers of America, who shepherded the project and pulled it all together; and Ivy Fischer Stone of the Fifi Oscard Agency, who got the book off the ground; finally, the active members of the Mystery Writers of America, for their enthusiastic cooperation.

Introduction

✦✦

Peter Ginna and Jane Cavolina, Crown Publishers, Inc.

What's the greatest mystery of all time? Without a doubt, it's got to be *The Nine Tailors*.

No, wait a minute, surely it's *The Daughter of Time*.

Excuse me, but aren't you forgetting *The Maltese Falcon*?

How can it not be *The Hound of the Baskervilles*?

What about *Crime and Punishment*? That's a mystery, too.

Everybody loves to talk about their favorite mysteries, including us. We've spent many an hour arguing Agatha Christie's plots versus P. D. James's characterizations, Ed McBain's procedural detail versus George V. Higgins's dialogue. Nobody can prove one book is the greatest mystery of all time, but everybody has a favorite. Part of the fun of having these conversations with other mystery readers is learning about mysteries you've never read, and going off and discovering them for yourself. The other part of the fun is just arguing.

We decided to ask the most informed mystery lovers, the members of the Mystery Writers of America, to pick their favorite mysteries. We then asked them to go one step further and choose their favorites in ten categories: classics, suspense, hardboiled/private eye, police procedural, espionage/thriller, criminal, cozy/traditional, historical, humorous, and legal/courtroom. And while we were at it, we asked them to vote on various other things: Their favorite authors and sleuths, male and female, their favorite murder weapon, and their favorite hiding place for a body (we were curious). Then we threw in a list of writers and their works that have won (or been nominated for) the coveted Edgar, awarded each year by the members of the MWA.

The Crown Crime Companion is the result. It may introduce you to some books you haven't read, and it certainly will inspire you to re-read some you have. We hope it starts as many good arguments for you as it has for us!

MICKEY FRIEDMAN

P.S. The greatest mystery ever written is undoubtedly *And Then There Were None.*—J.C.

P.P.S. The greatest mystery ever written is without question *The High Window.*—P.G.

Making the Lists: A Saga

MICKEY FRIEDMAN

It sounded easy. Since I was at that time publications chair of the Mystery Writers of America, I agreed to put together the lists that form the basis of the *Crime Companion*. I would sent out a questionnaire to active MWA members (i.e., those published in the mystery field), asking them to pick their fifty favorite mysteries—five in each of ten categories. The titles that got most votes overall would be the Top 100. The top ten vote-getters within each category would make up the list of category favorites. All I had to do was gather the returned questionnaires from the MWA office and tabulate the results.

Well, it sounded *relatively* easy.

I will pass lightly over the agony of setting up the categories, a task shared by Crown editors Jane Cavolina and Peter Ginna, MWA literary agent Ivy Stone, Otto Penzler, and me. If you have never tried to fasten down a rushing stream with an iron grid, you probably won't appreciate what we went through. When we had at last decided on Classics, Suspense, Hard-boiled/Private Eye, Police Procedural, Espionage/Thriller, Criminal, Cozy/Traditional, Historical, Humorous, and Legal/Courtroom, I put together the questionnaire.

The questionnaire was mailed to active MWA members along with an arm-twisting memo from me, begging them to fill it out. I trumpeted, "We intend to produce a volume that will be fun to read, a splendid gift, a book that will send anyone who comes across it, whether mystery novice or aficionado, to the nearest bookstore or library screaming for mysteries." The membership bought it. The completed questionnaires—representing, I should mention, a major investment of time for those who filled them out—began to arrive. In the end we had upwards of two hundred.

Then the fun began.

It is common, when making acknowledgments, to give a nice little "without whom" pat on the back to one's spouse. In this case the simple truth is that without the stalwart assistance and computer expertise of my husband, Alan Friedman, I would still be floundering and there would be no lists even now. During the course of a four-day Memorial Day weekend, the two of us worked all day every day and stayed up until three or four every morning—tabulating, tabulating, tabulating.

The procedure was this: First, by hand, we went through every questionnaire and wrote down every single book mentioned. We ended up with a list of 2,090 titles by 880 authors. (Many choices were annotated by vociferous notes. Obviously, the respondents had become passionately involved in the project.)

Using this master list, we created a database on the computer, noting each title and the number of votes it received in each of the ten categories.

Then the computer calculated the total number of votes each book got in each category and the total in all categories. The highest vote-getters, regardless of category, make up the Top 100.

Since many books were mentioned in more than one category, our next step was to assign each book to a single category. We decided it made sense to put a title in the category in which it had received the most votes. An example: *The Daughter of Time,* by Josephine Tey, was a very popular choice, but a choice many people found difficult to categorize. The book received votes in Suspense, Cozy/Traditional, Historical, and Humorous. The overwhelming majority listed it under Historical, however, so we moved all of its votes to the Historical category. All votes counted toward giving *The Daughter of Time* its number-four ranking in the Top 100.

By this time we had a preliminary list of which titles had gotten the most votes in each of the ten categories. We went through the category lists and picked out the top ten vote-getters in each. If there was a tie, we broke it by awarding the higher ranking to the author who had received the most votes on the overall list. (Our rationale was that some prolific authors, who had many titles mentioned in a category, were in effect splitting their own vote.)

At many points the process I have described resembled never-ending chaos. It was almost miraculous, toward the end, to see the lists begin to emerge out of the ooze. Even more exciting for me was to see what solid lists they turned out to be. I probably could come up with some quibbles—a favorite book slighted here, a not-so-favorite honored there—but on the whole I am delighted with the results and am proud that my days of drudgery produced something so worthwhile—a volume, I might even say, "that will be fun to read, a splendid gift, a book that will send anyone who comes across it, whether mystery novice or aficionado, to the nearest bookstore or library screaming for mysteries."

Part One

---◆◆---

THE LISTS

The Top 100 Mystery Novels of All Time

SELECTED BY ACTIVE MWA MEMBERS

1 · *THE COMPLETE SHERLOCK HOLMES*, Arthur Conan Doyle
Including these individual high vote-getters:
THE HOUND OF THE BASKERVILLES
A STUDY IN SCARLET
THE ADVENTURES OF SHERLOCK HOLMES
THE SIGN OF FOUR

2 · *THE MALTESE FALCON*, Dashiell Hammett

3 · *TALES OF MYSTERY AND IMAGINATION*, Edgar Allan Poe
Including these individual high vote-getters:
"THE GOLD BUG"
"THE MURDERS IN THE RUE MORGUE"

4 · *THE DAUGHTER OF TIME*, Josephine Tey

5 · *PRESUMED INNOCENT*, Scott Turow

6 · *THE SPY WHO CAME IN FROM THE COLD*, John le Carré

7 · *THE MOONSTONE*, Wilkie Collins

8 · *THE BIG SLEEP*, Raymond Chandler

9 · *REBECCA*, Daphne du Maurier

10 · *AND THEN THERE WERE NONE*, Agatha Christie

11 · *ANATOMY OF A MURDER*, Robert Traver

12 · *THE MURDER OF ROGER ACKROYD*, Agatha Christie

13 · *THE LONG GOODBYE*, Raymond Chandler

14 · *THE POSTMAN ALWAYS RINGS TWICE*, James M. Cain

15 · *THE GODFATHER*, Mario Puzo

16 · *THE SILENCE OF THE LAMBS*, Thomas Harris

17 · *A COFFIN FOR DIMITRIOS*, Eric Ambler

18 · *GAUDY NIGHT*, Dorothy L. Sayers

19 · *WITNESS FOR THE PROSECUTION*, Agatha Christie

20 · *THE DAY OF THE JACKAL*, Frederick Forsyth

21 · *FAREWELL, MY LOVELY*, Raymond Chandler

22 · *THE THIRTY-NINE STEPS*, John Buchan

23 · *THE NAME OF THE ROSE*, Umberto Eco

24 · *CRIME AND PUNISHMENT*, Fyodor Dostoevksi

25 · *EYE OF THE NEEDLE*, Ken Follett

26 · *RUMPOLE OF THE BAILEY*, John Mortimer

27 · *RED DRAGON*, Thomas Harris

28 · *THE NINE TAILORS*, Dorothy L. Sayers

29 · *FLETCH*, Gregory Mcdonald

30 · *TINKER, TAILOR, SOLDIER, SPY*, John le Carré

31 · *THE THIN MAN*, Dashiell Hammett

32 · *THE WOMAN IN WHITE*, Wilkie Collins

33 · *TRENT'S LAST CASE*, E. C. Bentley

34 · *DOUBLE INDEMNITY*, James M. Cain

35 · *GORKY PARK*, Martin Cruz Smith

36 · *STRONG POISON*, Dorothy L. Sayers

37 · *DANCE HALL OF THE DEAD*, Tony Hillerman

38 · *THE HOT ROCK*, Donald E. Westlake

39 · *RED HARVEST*, Dashiell Hammett

40 · *THE CIRCULAR STAIRCASE*, Mary Roberts Rinehart

41 · *MURDER ON THE ORIENT EXPRESS*, Agatha Christie

42 · *THE FIRM*, John Grisham

43 · *THE IPCRESS FILE*, Len Deighton

44 · *LAURA*, Vera Caspary

45 · *I, THE JURY*, Mickey Spillane

46 · *THE LAUGHING POLICEMAN*, Maj Sjöwall and Per Wahlöö

47 · *BANK SHOT*, Donald E. Westlake

48 · *THE THIRD MAN*, Graham Greene

49 · *THE KILLER INSIDE ME*, Jim Thompson

50 · *WHERE ARE THE CHILDREN?* Mary Higgins Clark

51 · *"A" IS FOR ALIBI*, Sue Grafton

52 · *THE FIRST DEADLY SIN*, Lawrence Sanders

53 · *A THIEF OF TIME*, Tony Hillerman

54 · *IN COLD BLOOD*, Truman Capote

55 · *ROGUE MALE*, Geoffrey Household

56 · *MURDER MUST ADVERTISE*, Dorothy L. Sayers

57 · *THE INNOCENCE OF FATHER BROWN*, G. K. Chesterton

58 · *SMILEY'S PEOPLE*, John le Carré

59 · *THE LADY IN THE LAKE*, Raymond Chandler

60 · *TO KILL A MOCKINGBIRD*, Harper Lee

61 · *OUR MAN IN HAVANA*, Graham Greene

62 · *THE MYSTERY OF EDWIN DROOD*, Charles Dickens

63 · *WOBBLE TO DEATH*, Peter Lovesey

64 · *ASHENDEN*, W. Somerset Maugham

65 · *THE SEVEN PER-CENT SOLUTION*, Nicholas Meyer

66 · *THE DOORBELL RANG*, Rex Stout

67 · *STICK*, Elmore Leonard

68 · *THE LITTLE DRUMMER GIRL*, John le Carré

69 · *BRIGHTON ROCK*, Graham Greene

70 · *DRACULA*, Bram Stoker

71 · *THE TALENTED MR. RIPLEY*, Patricia Highsmith

72 · *THE MOVING TOYSHOP*, Edmund Crispin

73 · *A TIME TO KILL*, John Grisham

74 · *LAST SEEN WEARING*, Hillary Waugh

75 · *LITTLE CAESAR*, W. R. Burnett

76 · *THE FRIENDS OF EDDIE COYLE*, George V. Higgins

77 · *CLOUDS OF WITNESS*, Dorothy L. Sayers

78 · *FROM RUSSIA, WITH LOVE*, Ian Fleming

79 · *BEAST IN VIEW*, Margaret Millar

80 · *SMALLBONE DECEASED*, Michael Gilbert

81 · *THE FRANCHISE AFFAIR*, Josephine Tey

82 · *CROCODILE ON THE SANDBANK*, Elizabeth Peters

83 · *SHROUD FOR A NIGHTINGALE*, P. D. James

84 · *THE HUNT FOR RED OCTOBER*, Tom Clancy

85 · *CHINAMAN'S CHANCE*, Ross Thomas

86 · *THE SECRET AGENT*, Joseph Conrad

87 · *THE DREADFUL LEMON SKY*, John D. MacDonald

88 · *THE GLASS KEY*, Dashiell Hammett

89 · *JUDGMENT IN STONE*, Ruth Rendell

90 · *BRAT FARRAR*, Josephine Tey

91 · *THE CHILL*, Ross Macdonald

92 · *DEVIL IN A BLUE DRESS*, Walter Mosley

93 · *THE CHOIRBOYS*, Joseph Wambaugh

94 · *GOD SAVE THE MARK*, Donald E. Westlake

95 · *HOME SWEET HOMICIDE*, Craig Rice

96 · *THE THREE COFFINS*, John Dickson Carr

97 · *PRIZZI'S HONOR*, Richard Condon

98 · *THE STEAM PIG*, James McClure

99 · *TIME AND AGAIN*, Jack Finney

100 · *A MORBID TASTE FOR BONES*, Ellis Peters, and *ROSEMARY'S BABY*, Ira Levin (TIE)

1. · *THE COMPLETE SHERLOCK HOLMES*
BY Arthur Conan Doyle · (1887–1927)

*R*ightly elected to the number one slot as the most distinguished mystery fiction ever written, the Sherlock Holmes canon stands alone as the most consistently brilliant, original, important, and entertaining works of fiction ever produced. While four books received numerous votes, *The Hound of the Baskervilles, A Study in Scarlet, The Adventures of Sherlock Holmes,* and *The Sign of Four,* it is impossible to separate one book from another, as the nine volumes (four novels and 56 short stories) all form part of a greater whole, as the Charlie Chan movies and the episodes of *Cheers* and the ingredients of a bouillabaisse cannot be examined individually for an accurate sense of the complete oeuvre.

Holmes, the brilliant, eccentric private detective, lives with his friend and chronicler, Dr. John H. Watson, who perfectly serves as the foil for Holmes's extraordinary observations and the deductions he makes from them. As clients visit the famous sitting room at 221B Baker Street, they bring outré tales that entice the easily bored Holmes to solve curious puzzles and heinous crimes.

In *The Hound of the Baskervilles* an infamous ancient family legend of a phantom hound appears to have a strong element of truth in the present day when one member of the Baskerville family is murdered and another is in imminent danger.

A Study in Scarlet, the first Holmes adventure, tells the story of a Mormon vendetta. In *The Sign of Four* a fabulous Indian treasure leads to many murders. Of the twelve stories in *the Adventures of Sherlock Holmes,* none is more famous than the first, "A Scandal in Bohemia," in which Holmes admits to being outsmarted by Irene Adler, always referred to as "*the* woman" by the smitten sleuth. Other great mysteries solved include "The Red-Headed League," "The Speckled Band," and "The Five Orange Pips."

The other books about Holmes—by Doyle only, there being many hundreds by other authors—are *The Valley of Fear* (regarded by some as the best Holmes novel of them all), *The Memoirs of*

Sherlock Holmes, The Return of Sherlock Holmes, His Last Bow, and *The Casebook of Sherlock Holmes.* There have been more than a hundred movies starring Holmes and innumerable radio, television, and theatrical performances.

2. · *THE MALTESE FALCON*
BY Dashiell Hammett · (1930)

The only novel in which the famous Sam Spade appears, regarded by many as Hammett's finest work, this is possibly the best American detective novel ever written. Whatever its merits, this book and the two earlier Hammett novels established the American hard-boiled private-eye novel as a subgenre of crime fiction unique to the United States, often attempted by writers in other countries who invariably produced pale, silly, and generally misguided failures, unable to capture the sense of individuality, toughness, and honor exemplified by the American P.I.

When Spade's partner is gunned down on a case, he figures he ought to do something about it, even though he has no affection for him and had been having an affair with his wife. Masquerading as Miss Wonderly, the gorgeous redhead later identified as Brigid O'Shaughnessy hires the firm of Spade and Archer to folllow a man. Spade quickly becomes caught up in a frantic search for a statue of immense value, a jewel-encrusted bird worth millions, and avidly sought by Caspar Gutman, the fat man, and his henchmen.

While everyone knows the superior 1941 film written and directed by John Huston, that was the third version of *The Maltese Falcon.* The first, released in 1931, starred Ricardo Cortez as Spade and Bebe Daniels as Brigid. *Satan Met a Lady* starred Warren William as urbane Spade, renamed Ted Shayne, and Bette Davis as the treacherous O'Shaughnessy. In the great version, of course, Humphrey Bogart immortalized Spade, Mary Astor did the same for Brigid, and Sydney Greenstreet was perfect as Gutman.

3. · TALES OF MYSTERY AND IMAGINATION
BY Edgar Allan Poe · (1845)

*I*t is a well-recorded, and relatively accurate, fact that Poe defined the detective story in just three tales and since then all other detective stories have been merely variations.

Oddly, neither of the two stories that were heavy vote-getters is Poe's best story. "The Gold Bug" is not a detective story at all but an old-fashioned deciphering of a cryptogram in a tale without a crime.

"The Murders in the Rue Morgue" (1841) introduced C. Auguste Dupin, literature's first true detective. In this story Poe also created the slightly stupid sidekick (who assumes the role of the reader as he asks questions so that the brilliant detective can explain). The dull, ineffectual policeman is here as well, along with the bizarre, apparently impossible, crime. Clues are neatly hidden and a red herring obfuscates the trail.

Poe's other two mysteries, not heavily named by voters but collected in *Tales,* are "The Mystery of Marie Roget," Dupin's entirely cerebral reconstruction and solution of a crime (based on the real-life murder in New York of Mary Rogers) from his analysis of newspaper clippings, and "The Purloined Letter," his finest work, in which Dupin recovers a stolen document that could be sufficiently embarrassing to bring down a government.

More famous for his dark tales of terror and the supernatural, Poe's work has engendered scores of films, a few of which are classics of horror.

4. · THE DAUGHTER OF TIME
BY Josephine Tey · (1951)

*O*ne of the few mystery classics that has actually been read by those who praise it, this tour de force remains a masterpiece of construction and pure detection with few rivals in the history of the genre.

Scotland Yard inspector Alan Grant is severely injured in the line of duty and goes to the hospital. Since it appears that his stay will be a long one, he engages in a cerebral exercise to help pass the time, examining the famous accusation that Richard III murdered his two nephews in the Tower of London. Although history has laid the crime at the king's feet, Grant is convinced of his innocence and, by analyzing the known information, he proves that someone else was responsible for the death of the young boys.

The Daughter of Time, defined by an old proverb is, of course, truth.

5. · *PRESUMED INNOCENT*
BY Scott Turow · (1987)

*I*t is uncommon in the history of mystery fiction for a single book to have so major an influence on the genre as this one did—not because of its style or viewpoint but because of its plot. The extraordinary success of this flawed but riveting courtroom novel (one of the bestselling mysteries of all time) immediately sent readers and, necessarily, publishers in search of more legal thrillers. There have been more than a few since that search began.

A beautiful and sexy young lawyer is raped and murdered. A colleague who had been passionately obsessed with her is arrested for her murder. Everything in his life—his career, his marriage, his freedom—is at stake, and the prosecution appears to have an airtight case. Only his wife continues to have faith in him. Or does she?

An excellent film version of the book starred Harrison Ford.

6. · *THE SPY WHO CAME IN FROM THE COLD*
BY John le Carré · (1963)

*E*spionage fiction has proven to be more volatile than detective fiction, partially because while the world changes, country gardens and mean streets don't. But every so often a spy novel appears and changes all of the spy novels written after it. *The Spy Who Came in from the Cold* is one of these seminal works, bringing a new level of cynicism and gloom to the form while forever defining the sphere of agents as one colored in shades of gray, not the black-and-white heroes and villains we had come to expect.

George Smiley, who went on to become the character most familiar to le Carré readers, plays only a minor role in the story of Alec Leamas, a British agent sent over the wall into East Germany to bring out a valuable source of information: a former Nazi counterspy. Leamas has no idea that a much bigger game is being played and that he is merely a pawn in a giant East-West struggle. He is doomed, willingly giving up his life though he has long since stopped believing in the cause to which he has become a martyr.

A superb 1965 film version starred Richard Burton, Claire Bloom, and Oskar Werner.

7. · *THE MOONSTONE*
BY Wilkie Collins · (1868)

*T*S. Elliott described Collins's famous Victorian novel as "the first, the longest and the best" mystery ever written. He was wrong on all three counts, but the statement reflects the justly high regard in which the great Victorian novel is held.

Soon after Rachel Verinder receives a priceless moonstone from Franklin Blake on her birthday, she reports it missing from her room. When the local police are unable to recover it, Blake wires Scotland Yard and Sergeant Cuff, the finest detective in England, arrives and discovers a smudge on Rachel's freshly painted door. When she refuses to permit a search for the stained garment, Cuff suspects her of having staged the theft and quits the case. Rachel, who has fallen in love with Blake, nevertheless treats him so abominably after the loss of the gem that he leaves England. Rachel's maid commits suicide and leaves a note for Blake in which she reveals that her mistress suspected him of being the thief. He returns, with Sergeant Cuff, to solve the case.

8. · *THE BIG SLEEP*
BY Raymond Chandler · (1939)

*T*his book, by the author generally regarded as the finest mystery writer produced by America in the twentieth century, marks the first appearance of Philip Marlowe.

General Sternwood, old, paralyzed, and gravely ill, hires the Los Angeles private detective to help one of his two daughters. Immoral and drug-addicted, the retired general's younger daughter is being blackmailed for posing for nude photographs. Although surrounded by corruption and deceit, Marlowe remains a powerful moral force in his quixotic attempts to find truth and abet justice.

The Big Sleep, Chandler's metaphor for death, was made into a popular hard-boiled movie starring Humphrey Bogart, Lauren Bacall, and James Stewart, with the screenplay by William Faulkner.

9. · *REBECCA*
BY Daphne du Maurier · (1938)

" "*L*ast night I dreamt I went to Manderley again." The opening line of perhaps the greatest romantic suspense novel ever written has become as familiar to readers as "Call me Ishmael" from *Moby-Dick.*

The great Cornwall mansion is the setting for the appalling tension confronting Maxim de Winter's plain, gentle new wife. His coolness, combined with the silent hostility of Mrs. Danvers, the grim housekeeper who had been devoted to Rebecca, Max's first wife, tortures the insecure and frightened young bride as she tries to unlock the secret of Manderley and the death of Rebecca.

The film that starred Laurence Olivier and Joan Fontaine is one of Alfred Hitchcock's masterpieces.

10. · *AND THEN THERE WERE NONE*
BY Agatha Christie · (1939)

*O*ne of the many tours de force by arguably the greatest mystery plotter who ever lived, this suspense classic is unusual for Dame Agatha since it is not a detective story but rather a thriller about a serial killer. The dénouement reaches a new height with regard to the least likely suspect.

In this now familiar story, ten people—each with a secret in their past—are invited to a lavish mansion on an otherwise uninhabited island from which no one can leave. Their mysterious host does not greet his guests personally but communicates with them via recorded messages. Terror mounts as the trapped visitors are murdered, one by one, in a fashion suggested by the old nursery rhyme.

Originally titled *Ten Little Niggers* in England and published as *Ten Little Indians* in the United States, the book has been filmed several times, most notably in 1945 with Barry Fitzgerald, Louis Hayward, Walter Huston, and Judith Anderson.

11. · *ANATOMY OF A MURDER*
BY Robert Traver · (1958)

*I*n spite of the breathtaking successes of Erle Stanley Gardner, Scott Turow, and John Grisham, it is entirely possible that the best and most realistic courtroom novel of all is *Anatomy of a Murder.*

Based on a true incident, it is the story of a sexy young woman who hires Paul Biegler, a semiretired lawyer, to defend her husband. She tells Biegler that she was raped by Barney Quill, a barkeep, and when she returned home beaten and violated, her husband, army lieutenant Frederick Manion, found Quill and shot him three times. At the trial Biegler's defense is that Manion had an "irresistible impulse." The prosecutor suggests that Laura Manion and Quill were lovers, that Manion caught them and beat his wife and shot her boyfriend. The jury announces its decision based on the temporary insanity plea, and the ambivalent ending remains as shocking today as when the book was first published.

Otto Preminger made one of his greatest movies from the best-selling novel in 1959, featuring a superb cast with James Stewart, Lee Remick, Ben Gazzara, and George C. Scott.

12. · *THE MURDER OF ROGER ACKROYD*
BY Agatha Christie · (1926)

*R*egarded by many as the greatest plotter that the history of detective fiction ever produced, and unlikely to be matched, Agatha Christie offered readers her most controversial novel, which lent its name to Edmund Wilson's infamous attack on mysteries: "Who Cares Who Killed Roger Ackroyd?" Although clues are fairly sprinkled throughout the book, the least-likely-person convention is raised to a previously unheard of, and doubtlessly unthought of, level.

Dr. James Sheppard narrates this tale about the unusually violent murder of Roger Ackroyd, for which Hercule Poirot comes out of a retirement that has lasted more than two decades. Although half a dozen people had both motive and opportunity to commit the crime, circumstantial evidences brands the guilty party. Only the great Belgian detective remains unconvinced.

The Ackroyd case was the first of Agatha Christie's books to be filmed. Austin Trevor starred in the 1931 film, which was titled *Alibi*.

13. · *THE LONG GOODBYE*
BY Raymond Chandler · (1954)

*P*erhaps the greatest of Chandler's novels, and certainly the most cynical, it features an older, maybe wiser Philip Marlowe who trusts no one and encounters only people who are corrupt, greedy, and cruel.

Thanks to plastic surgery, Terry Lennox has a new face, but he also has a new problem. He has to get across the border to Mexico because he thinks he might have killed somebody, although he isn't sure. He hires Marlowe to find out the truth, and the private eye quickly learns that Lennox had nothing to do with the murder. But Lennox's troubles are far from over.

A surprisingly good adaptation, despite the miscasting of Elliott Gould as Marlowe, was filmed in 1973.

14. · *THE POSTMAN ALWAYS RINGS TWICE*
BY James M. Cain · (1934)

*T*his depression-era masterpiece is typical of Cain's hard-boiled crime fiction in that it shows crime and its consequences from the viewpoint of the criminal.

Frank Chambers is driven nearly mad with desire for Cora, the beautiful and sexy young wife of Nick Papadalis, who hired the out-of-work Frank to work in his diner. When Cora decides she wants Nick out of her life—permanently—her lover is drawn inexorably into murder.

Lana Turner and John Garfield were cast as the passionate and doomed couple in the first film version of this *noir* novel; Jessica Lange and Jack Nicholson reprised the steamy relationship nearly four decades later.

15. · *THE GODFATHER*
BY Mario Puzo · (1969)

*W*ith a single massive volume, Puzo forever changed the gangster novel and the public perception of the Mafia. Previously gangsters were portrayed as individuals who were tougher or smarter (rarely both) than their adversaries, who were mainly cops and G-men. In Puzo's portrait gangsters were seen as part of a family, generally with deep roots and many members who are ruthless businessmen. The novel quickly became hugely successful all around the world, and for many years held the number one spot as the bestselling crime novel of all time.

The Corleone family, working in relative peace with other Mafia families, is thriving under the guidance of Don Vito. When a rival family shoots him down, one of his sons is expected to take over as head of the family. Sonny is ambitious and violent, eager to avenge his father's death. Fredo is a weakling who wants the perks of being at the top of a powerful hierarchy. Michael has no desire to live a life of crime. But when his brothers prove unequal to the job—Sonny because of his violent temper and Fredo because of his disloyalty—Michael calmly assumes command.

It is impossible to think of *The Godfather* without considering the superb films that it inspired. *The Godfather* (1972) and *The Godfather, Part II* (1975) each won numerous Oscars and starred Al Pacino, Marlon Brando, Robert Duvall, Diane Keaton, James Caan, and Robert De Niro. *Part III,* also excellent, did not receive quite the same overwhelming acclaim.

16. · *THE SILENCE OF THE LAMBS*
BY Thomas Harris · (1988)

*I*t is possible to count on one's fingers those rare occasions when a nearly perfect book inspires a nearly perfect film, but such is the case with *The Silence of the Lambs,* one of the greatest thrillers ever written. The author has only written three books, but each is a classic. His first thriller, *Black Sunday,* is one of the half-dozen best terrorist novels, and his second, *Red Dragon,* also appears on this list.

A maniacal serial killer—known as "Buffalo Bill" because of his penchant for skinning his victims—abducts and murders young women. Clarice Starling, a young FBI trainee, is drawn into the case. Her involvement brings her face-to-face with Hannibal Lecter, the most diabolical criminal genius in the prison system. In return for small favors Lecter promises to help the ambitious agent capture the killer. Can a totally evil man be trusted?

Jonathan Demme's 1990 movie starred Jodie Foster in her greatest role, and Anthony Hopkins's Lecter is so memorably convincing that his image lingers long after the film has ended.

17. · *A COFFIN FOR DIMITRIOS*
BY Eric Ambler · (1939)

*S*urely the most famous and possibly the best of Ambler's many distinguished novels, *A Coffin for Dimitrios* represents one of the milestones of espionage fiction and brought it truly and irrevocably into the modern era. Average people behaving bravely, albeit through no desire of their own, as events threaten and engulf them is the hallmark of Ambler's thrillers.

The sad and squalid death of Dimitrios Makropoulos interests author Charles Latimer, whose curiosity is slightly slaked by Turkish policeman Colonel Haki. As Latimer delves more deeply into the multinational criminal life of the murdered Greek, he comes to realize that Haki is using him to uncover more and more details of Makropoulos's espionage activities, exposing him to dangers he had never anticipated.

The 1944 film version starred Zachary Scott, Sydney Greenstreet, and Peter Lorre.

18. · *GAUDY NIGHT*
BY Dorothy L. Sayers · (1935)

*C*elebrated for being a practically crimeless crime novel, *Gaudy Night* is, above all, a story of relationships and of human nature, with an emphasis on the choices women must make in a world beset by change. For passionate Sayers fans, its most significant moment comes when Harriet at last agrees to marry Peter.

Harriet Vane, bluestocking mystery writer and onetime murder suspect, takes flight once again from the unwanted (or so she wishes to believe) ardor of her suitor, Lord Peter Wimsey. Her temporary refuge is the familiar female environment of Shrewsbury, her old Oxford college, where the annual reunion, or "gaudy," is in progress. However, she finds the cherished atmosphere of intellectual fellowship poisoned by some spiteful presence lurking unidentified amidst the resident and returning scholars.

19. · *WITNESS FOR THE PROSECUTION*
BY Agatha Christie · (1948)

*A*s worthy as this brilliant courtroom thriller is, it should not have been ranked as one of the top 100 mystery books because, well, there is no such book. Those who voted for it presumably remember the superb stage play, the equally superb movie, or the excellent short story on which they were both based (though the story's ending is quite different from that of the dramatic presentations).

When a charming young man is arrested for murdering a wealthy widow, the chief witness against him is his wife. But after the trial begins, a bundle of love letters is given to his defense attorney by a London prostitute, throwing suspicion on the wife's motivations.

Surely one of the half-dozen best mystery plays ever written,

Witness for the Prosecution opened in London in 1953 and won the New York Drama Critics Circle Award as the best foreign play of 1954–55. The memorable film of 1957 starred Tyrone Power, Marlene Dietrich, Charles Laughton, and Elsa Lanchester.

20. · *THE DAY OF THE JACKAL*
BY Frederick Forsyth · (1971)

*I*t seems virtually impossible for a suspense story to succeed when the ending is already known. The entire notion is antithetical to the very point of suspense fiction. Yet that is the enormous hurdle that needs to be overcome when an author uses a well-known historical figure and presents a fictional scenario that cannot end his life when history records that he lived beyond that point.

An anonymous Englishman, code-named Jackal, takes a dangerous but lucrative contract. The fee is a half-million dollars. His target is Charles de Gaulle, the president of France. He has a foolproof plan. But the most brilliant counterespionage agents in Europe set up their own foolproof plan to trap him but fail. The intellectual chess match, with the future of the world at stake, is meticulously detailed and it is so believable that it is difficult to believe that this terrifying novel is not a massive journalistic report.

A splendid motion picture was directed by Fred Zinnemann in 1973, with Edward Fox in the eponymous role.

21. · *FAREWELL, MY LOVELY*
BY Raymond Chandler · (1940)

*C*handler, the poet laureate of the American hard-boiled detective novel, provides one of his most interesting supporting casts for Philip Marlowe, the white knight of crime fiction, in the second adventure of the Los Angeles private eye.

Marlowe is stopped outside a Negro bar by Moose Malloy, who grabs him with "a hand I could have sat in" and takes him upstairs to find his old girlfriend, Velma, who is "as cute as lace pants." When the P.I. sets out to find little Velma, he encounters a charlatan who calls himself a psychic, a gorgeous blonde with everything except morals, a gambler, an Indian with the shoulders of a blacksmith and the legs of a chimpanzee, an honest cop, several dishonest ones, and murder.

Murder, My Sweet, the retitled Dick Powell vehicle, became the first Marlowe feature in 1944; it also starred Claire Trevor and Mike Mazurki as Moose. Strangely, two years earlier the book had also served as the basis for a simplified screen adaptation as *The Falcon Takes Over.*

22. · *THE THIRTY-NINE STEPS*
BY John Buchan · (1915)

*A*s exciting a thriller today as it was when it was written, this classic chase tale is now most remembered for the superb Alfred Hitchcock movie of 1935, starring Robert Donat and Madeleine Carroll.

Richard Hannay, a former army officer, is approached by a mysterious woman who is later found murdered in his room. The police think he killed her and foreign spies believe she passed a vital secret to him, so both groups want him, chasing him across the Scottish terrain until he is able to discover the secret and prove his innocence.

23. · *THE NAME OF THE ROSE*
BY Umberto Eco · (1980)

*T*his surprise international bestseller, translated from the Italian, is a grab bag of medieval scholarship and postmodernist playfulness. With its endless quotations in Greek, Latin, Hebrew, etc., it qualifies as the least-read bestseller of its time, rivaled only by Stephen Hawking's *A Brief History of Time*. Purporting to be an actual first-person memoir relating "the terrible story of Adso of Melk," it tells in a carefully arranged account spanning seven days, with each day separated into the liturgical hours, how Adso, a young Benedictine novice, was once witness to monkish murder and mayhem. At the heart of the mystery, which alternates a more or less straightforward amateur detective's narrative with pedagogical and philosophical digressions, lies a tantalizing but elusive manuscript: a copy of Aristotle's lost treatise on comedy.

French director Jean-Jacques Annaud brought this fourteenth-century crime fantasy to the screen in a somber and overrespectful 1986 film starring Sean Connery.

24. · CRIME AND PUNISHMENT
BY Fyodor Dostoevski · (1866)

*A*ll the classic elements of the mystery novel are present in this unrelentingly dark tale: theft, murder, a second murder to cover the initial crime, a murderer, a detective, clues, pursuit, and ultimately, an arrest. The major distinction of this classic, apart from the elevated literary style of the author, is that the murderer is punished, via his own crushing sense of guilt, *before* his apprehension.

Raskolnikov, a poor student, murders a pawnbroker and then the greedy old man's sister when she catches him. Although he escapes, a clever policeman, Petrovich, suspects him and hounds him relentlessly until his conscience forces him to confess.

Peter Lorre played the tormented Raskolnikov in a 1935 film version.

25. · *EYE OF THE NEEDLE*
BY Ken Follett · (1978)

A writer with several unsuccessful books written under various pseudonyms, Ken Follett hit on a splendid idea for a thriller and produced *Storm Island,* as this book was called in the U.K. His subsequent work has kept the author on bestseller lists around the world. Known as one of the most popular espionage writers, his finest work, however, is the huge historical saga *Pillars of the Earth.*

A handsome, aristocratic German spy of great intelligence learns a secret that could win the war for Hitler. The only person who may be able to stop him is a beautiful young Englishwoman who lives a lonely life on a barren island with her wheelchair-bound husband. "The Needle" is ruthless, but he is drawn to the lovely Lucy. She is filled with desire but knows her duty. Which deeply felt emotions will prevail?

Richard Marquand directed the 1981 film that starred Donald Sutherland.

26. · *RUMPOLE OF THE BAILEY*
BY John Mortimer · (1978)

K nown as much for his bibulousness as for his dubious legal tricks and canny bursts of intuition, Horace Rumpole, barrister-at-law, appears in only one novel-length work but enlivens several books of short stories of which this was the first. His many cases, which derive their characteristic flavor from Mortimer's deadpan style and droll portrait of his hero's predictable idiosyncrasies, feature criminal behavior that ranges from the merely larcenous to the seriously nasty. The supporting cast includes Rumpole's fellow regulars at Pommeroy's Wine Bar, so convenient to the Inns of Court, as well as the redoubtable Mrs. Horace Rumpole, better known to delighted readers as "She Who Must Be Obeyed."

The Rumpole stories are a marvelous exception in the often

less than satisfactory symbiotic relationship between televised crime fiction and its published counterpart. Originally scripted as a British television vehicle for veteran character actor Leo McKern, Mortimer's hour-long plays actually gained in literary stature when, enhanced by greater detail and humorous flourishes, they made the transition to the printed page.

27. · *RED DRAGON*
BY Thomas Harris · (1981)

*P*erhaps the finest violent suspense novel ever written, *Red Dragon* introduces Hannibal Lecter, certainly the most memorable villain in modern literature. Harris somehow manages to create the perfect evil genius without reducing him to a cartoon figure, regardless of Julian Symons's assertions to the contrary. Even in jail Hannibal "The Cannibal" is chillingly dangerous, and his brief appearances in this novel and in *The Silence of the Lambs* are among the most heart-pounding in crime fiction.

A ferocious serial killer commits the most vicious crimes imaginable: murdering, torturing, ripping apart his victims. Men, women, children—entire families are equally at risk. After all the the law-enforcement agencies fail to stop him, Will Graham is talked out of retirement by the FBI because of his special talent for understanding and capturing serial killers. He even managed to put Dr. Lecter behind bars. Graham discovers a connection between the deranged killer and Lecter, so he seeks help from the archfiend. When Graham learns that his family is vulnerable, he realizes that he may have made a terrible mistake.

A decent film version, titled *Manhunter* and directed by Michael Mann, was released in 1986.

28. · *THE NINE TAILORS*
BY Dorothy L. Sayers · (1934)

*S*ubtitled "Changes Rung on an Old Theme in Two Short Touches and Two Full Peals," this novel—Sayers's ninth, coincidentally, of those she wrote solo—mixes the art of detection with that of campanology, or bell ringing. Set in an East Anglian village resembling the one where Sayers had spent her childhood as a vicar's daughter, *The Nine Tailors* is at once intricately structured and yet grounded in the plain, deep-rooted spiritual traditions of rural England.

A road accident has deposited Lord Peter Wimsey and Bunter in isolated Fenchurch St. Paul one snowy New Year's Eve. In return for the hospitality extended, Wimsey allows himself to be drafted as a substitute bell ringer. Soon he is enmeshed in the darker secrets of the village, which include the puzzle of a mysterious mutilated corpse found in a grave not its own.

The phrase "nine tailors" refers to the number of peals signifying death: nine for a man, six for a woman.

29. · *FLETCH*
BY Gregory Mcdonald · (1974)

*I*n this first book of the series featuring the eponymous Irwin Fletcher, Mcdonald created a postsixties version of the likable but potentially dangerous freelance hero, a sort of synthesis of Travis McGee and Tom Ripley. An investigative reporter—in genre fiction always a useful choice of career, but more significant during the Watergate era when this book was conceived and published—Fletch emphatically doesn't play by the rules.

Approached about committing a capital crime, Fletch reacts ambiguously, repelled but still curious. He then spends the rest of the novel proving himself adept at turning the tables on each of his antagonists as they pop up to connive against him.

Two Fletch movies exist, both directed by Michael Ritchie and both featuring comic actor Chevy Chase in the title role. *Fletch,* the more successful of the two, was released in 1985, and *Fletch Lives* (which rightfully died at the box office) in 1989.

30. · TINKER, TAILOR, SOLDIER, SPY
BY John le Carré · (1974)

Although George Smiley appeared as the central figure in le Carré's first two novels, *Call for the Dead* and *A Murder of Quality,* where he functioned almost entirely as a detective, it is in this novel that he achieved his finest hour. While the novel is a pure masterpiece of espionage fiction, everything Smiley does is in the great tradition of observation and deduction employed by only the most distinguished detectives.

Because he is among the most trusted men in the British Secret Service, Smiley is given one of the most difficult tasks possible to assign to an agent: He must ferret out a counterspy. Karla, Smiley's counterpart in the espionage network of the Soviet Union, has successfully placed a mole in the British spy agency who has been intelligent and careful enough to work his way up to the very highest levels. Smiley must locate the traitor, even if it turns out to be a friend, a colleague, or a superior.

Alec Guinness successfully played Smiley in a six-part miniseries on the Public Broadcasting Service. The superb portrait was actually *too* successful; when le Carré saw it, he claimed that the character was no longer his own vision—that Smiley would forever be Guinness, and so le Carré decided to write no more about him.

31. · THE THIN MAN
BY Dashiell Hammett · (1934)

Although *The Thin Man* became enormously famous and beloved as a detective played by William Powell in six excellent films, in Hammett's book the titular character is the corpse, not the detective. Myrna Loy played Nora Charles in all of the films.

Nick Charles, the debonair playboy detective, tells everyone he married the fun-loving Nora for her money. When the couple arrives in New York for the Christmas holidays, Nora pushes Nick to get involved in a murder case involving his former client, the eccentric inventor Frank Wynant, who disappeared after his secretary was killed.

32. · *THE WOMAN IN WHITE*
BY Wilkie Collins · (1860)

*A*rguably the best Victorian novel involving crime and mystery, Collins's superb melodrama was one of the first to glorify the strong, intelligent, plain woman over the gentle, docile beauty.

Walter Hartright, on the way to his new position as drawing master to two young women, encounters Anne Catherick, a patient dressed all in white who has escaped from a nearby asylum. He then quickly falls in love with the younger of his students, the beautiful Laura Fairlie, in spite of her betrothal to the evil Sir Percival Clyde. Marian Halcombe, her half sister, learns of a plot by Clyde and his associate, the sinister Count Fosco, to steal Laura's fortune. When Hartright, who has left for Central America because of his impossible situation, learns that Laura has died, he returns to pay respects at her grave, only to discover that Laura is alive and Anne has been buried under the tombstone. With the courageous Marian, he sets out to avenge the evil done by the villains.

The Woman in White was filmed several times, most notably in 1948 with Vincent Price, Alexis Smith, Eleanor Parker, and Sydney Greenstreet perfectly cast as the unctuous Fosco.

33. · *TRENT'S LAST CASE*
BY E. C. Bentley · (1913)

*T*his landmark volume is notable for its tongue-in-cheek title (this being the detective's *first* case) and its groundbreaking attempt to tell about a very human detective rather than the superman-genius of the Sherlock Holmes variety. Often described as the first naturalistic detective novel, it ranks as a masterpiece for the brilliance of Philip Trent, the amateur detective, whose dazzling display of detection and deduction in the traditional dénouement has only one flaw—it is entirely wrong.

A wealthy financier has been murdered. Trent, a journalist, is sent to cover the story and, if possible, help solve the crime. He immediately falls in love with one of the most likely suspects.

Although seldom seen, *Trent's Last Case* has been filmed three times. The first was a silent movie starring Gregory Scott as Trent; Pauline Peters and Clive Brook co-starred. In 1929, Howard Hawks directed Raymond Griffith as Trent. The definitive version was released in 1953, with Michael Wilding as Trent, Orson Wells as the murdered millionaire, Sigsbee Manderson, and Margaret Lockwood as the love interest.

34. · *DOUBLE INDEMNITY*
BY James M. Cain · (1943)

*A*s he did in many of his books, Cain tells the story of an evil woman motivated by greed who corrupts a weak man motivated by lust. The noted critic Edmund Wilson called Cain and other American hard-boiled writers "poets of the tabloid murder."

A sexy woman uses her charms to seduce an insurance agent and schemes to kill her husband, making the murder look like an accident so that she can claim the double-indemnity payment. Only the company's claims adjuster, who suspects the freak train accident had been planned, stands in their way.

A memorable film version made in 1944 starred Fred Mac-
Murray, Barbara Stanwyck, and Edward G. Robinson.

35. · GORKY PARK
BY Martin Cruz Smith · (1981)

*G*orky Park became a byword for bestsellerdom by appearing
at exactly the right moment in time: the dawn of Ronald
Reagan's presidency. Smith spent a now legendary eight full years
on research in order to create with verisimilitude a story exploiting
the shabby pettiness of the Soviet bureaucracy and the blattered
humanity caught in its coils.

Chief homicide investigator Arkady Renko of the Moscow
town prosecutor's office is one of the officials called to the scene of
a triple slaying: three bodies, all wearing ice skates, their heads and
fingers missing, found under a layer of melting ice in popular
Gorky Park. Quickly taking charge of the case, Renko little realizes, as he tracks one pair of skates to its rightful owner, that his
involvement will change his life forever.

A film, which depended more on the story's dramatic Moscow
and New York settings for its impact than on its intense human
interactions, appeared in 1983. Directed by Michael Apted, it
starred William Hurt and Lee Marvin.

36. · STRONG POISON
BY Dorothy L. Sayers · (1930)

*S*ayers's second most famous creation, detective-novelist
Harriet Vane, is introduced in *Strong Poison,* and it is an
unforgettable moment. As the book opens, Harriet is on trial for
murder. Accused of killing her former lover, her motive, as stated
by the prosecution, is admittedly a peculiar one—that he behaved
like a cad by *asking* her to marry him. However, the most telling
strike against her is that she has recently purchased several poisons

in the name of literary research. Lord Peter Wimsey, a spectator in the courtroom, is intuitively convinced of her innocence and vows to clear her name, though, oddly enough, this gallant determination does not endear him to Harriet, who wishes neither to be pitied nor beholden.

It is a matter of record that Sayers, already worried about the intensity of her own relationship with her fictional hero, Lord Peter, began this fifth Wimsey novel with the plan to marry him off to Harriet and be done with him. Sayers's growing sense of the complexity of Harriet's nature worked against her intended conclusion, and the obviously smitten pair dueled romantically through several more novels before laying down their weapons in *Gaudy Night.*

37. · *DANCE HALL OF THE DEAD*
BY Tony Hillerman · (1973)

*I*n the second novel featuring Lt. Joe Leaphorn of the Navajo Tribal Police, a Suni Indian boy has been murdered and the suspected killer is a Navajo teenager only two years older. As is his custom, Hillerman, long an intimate observer of the Navajo and Pueblo environments, skillfully weaves into the familiar fabric of the police procedural exotic strands of tribal practice and myth. The result is a suspenseful unity of storytelling and culture, in which each part contributes equally to the pleasures of the whole.

However, there exists at least one exception to the generally approving Native American reaction to Hillerman's portrayal of their world. Recalling this instance, Hillerman, who was himself sent to an Indian boarding school, has said, ''In fact, the authenticity of ceremonial details . . . caused Zuni elders to cross-examine me about whether members of their kiva societies had revealed secrets to me.''

Dance Hall of the Dead won the Edgar as best novel of the year.

38. · *THE HOT ROCK*
BY Donald E. Westlake · (1970)

*T*he first novel featuring John Dortmunder and his gang remains one of the cornerstones of humorous mystery fiction, and the author remains the standard against which all other comic crime writers are measured.

A sacred jewel resides in the Brooklyn Museum and the representative of the African nation that claims ownership hires the Dortmunder gang to steal it and return it to its rightful owner. Dortmunder conceives a foolproof plan with his cohorts: Kelp, the 300-pound ''Tiny'' Belcher, and Murch, the best driver in town. When a small glitch in their plan occurs, they must steal the gem a second time. And a third. And they have to break *into* a prison.

William Goldman successfully adapted the novel for a screen version starring Robert Redford, George Segal, Ron Leibman, and Zero Mostel.

39. · *RED HARVEST*
BY Dashiell Hammett · (1929)

*A*lthough Hammett's most famous detectives are Sam Spade and Nick and Nora Charles, only the Continental Op appeared in more than one novel. The anonymous private eye also starred in *The Dain Curse*.

The Op travels to Personville, the mining town widely known as ''Poisonville'' because it is totally corrupt. His client, murdered the first night the dick is in town, is the first of numerous victims. When the Op learns that the police are as corrupt as the mob that controls the city, he sets them against each other in order to help clean up the place.

40. · THE CIRCULAR STAIRCASE
BY Mary Roberts Rinehart · (1908)

*P*roving that not all influences are positive, this enormously popular suspense novel may be regarded as mainly responsible for introducing the "Had-I-But Known" school of mystery fiction, in which the only common sense displayed is retrospective.

A young couple persuades their spinster aunt to rent a country house for the summer. Apparently well known to everyone within a radius of a day's journey (except, of course, to the innocent trio), valuable securities have been hidden in the walls of the house and there are some who will stop at nothing—including murder—to retrieve them.

The novel became the basis for the even more famous stage play, *The Bat,* which was co-authored with Avery Hopwood and which has been filmed several times, first as a 1926 silent, then as *The Bat Whispers* with Chester Morris and Una Merkel in 1930, and again as *The Bat* in 1959 with Agnes Moorehead and Vincent Price.

41. · MURDER ON THE ORIENT EXPRESS
BY Agatha Christie · (1934)

*I*t seems repetitive and/or redundant to describe yet another Christie novel as a tour de force with a brilliant variation on the least-likely-person scenario, but there is no choice with this opus. It was published in the U.S. with the far less evocative title *Murder in the Calais Coach.* Interestingly, Christie's husband, Max Mallowan, gave her the idea for the plot.

Hercule Poirot, the Belgian detective famous for the "little gray cells" he uses so effectively, is among the passengers on the famed train when its journey is halted by a snowstorm in Yugoslavia. Soon after the train becomes a snowbound prison, a murder occurs among the strange mix of international passengers.

Albert Finney successfully portrayed Poirot in the 1974 film with an all-star cast that included Lauren Bacall, Martin Balsam, Ingrid Bergman, Jacqueline Bisset, Sean Connery, John Gielgud, Anthony Perkins, and Richard Widmark.

42. · THE FIRM
BY John Grisham · (1991)

*I*t is almost impossible to think of *The Firm* without thinking of extraordinary numbers. The paperback version of *The Firm* was published in February 1992. Grisham's first book, *A Time to Kill,* had not yet had a mass-market paperback edition. Within eighteen months sales of those two titles, plus a third book, *The Pelican Brief,* surpassed twenty million copies in the U.S. alone, while also being monumental bestsellers around the world. No author in history has ever sold so many copies so quickly, not Stephen King, not Mickey Spillane, not Mario Puzo—no one.

An ambitious young lawyer is recruited by a prestigious firm, giving him immediate access to money, power, and success. He soon finds himself in trouble with the FBI and the law firm itself when he realizes that it is controlled by an organized-crime family.

Paramount produced a successful film in the summer of 1993, starring Tom Cruise and directed by Sydney Pollack.

43. · THE IPCRESS FILE
BY Len Deighton · (1962)

*A*lthough the character is unnamed in Deighton's hugely successful series of espionage novels in the 1960s, the reluctant spy—based largely on Ted Allbeury, a real-life British agent and bestselling espionage writer in his own right—was named Harry Palmer in the three movies that starred Michael Caine.

A small-time black marketeer is caught and given a choice: go to jail or work for the British Secret Service. He discovers an Iron

Curtain brainwashing center in the heart of London and exposes a formidable double agent.

44. · *LAURA*
BY Vera Caspary · (1942)

*W*as ever a good book better served by the film made from it than *Laura*? Memorable performances by Gene Tierney, Dana Andrews, and Clifton Webb as Waldo Lydecker and a haunting musical theme combine to make it a *noir* classic.

Detective Mark McPherson is assigned to the murder case of Laura Hunt and encounters Lydecker, New York's most famous columnist. The journalist talks of Laura so intimately that McPherson feels he has come to truly know her. Fascinated by the portrait of the beautiful girl, he finds himself inexplicably in love with her. It soon becomes clear that nothing is what it seems to be and another murder complicates the situation even further.

45. · *I, THE JURY*
BY Mickey Spillane · (1947)

*I*n the 1950s the hard-boiled detective novel was virtually moribund. Chandler wrote only two books, Hammett none, and Ross Macdonald was not yet read widely. Mickey Spillane filled the breach with the bestselling P.I. series in history.

The first Mike Hammer novel, *I, the Jury,* raised the level of toughness to new levels. The private eye hunts the killer of his old army friend, a man who lost his arm saving Hammer. When Hammer catches the killer, he remorselessly handles the execution himself. When the dying murderer asks, "How could you?" Hammer replies, "It was easy."

46. · *The Laughing Policeman*
by Maj Sjöwall and Per Wahlöö · (1970)

*M*ass murder, that ultimate act of chaos, is presented here against the backdrop of a determinedly orderly society. When nine people are slain on a Stockholm bus, it falls to Martin Beck of that city's homicide division to direct the investigation. The resulting narrative offers the authors' usual mix of Marxist dialectic, sourly potent social criticism, and unflashy detective work. Beck, plagued by a bad stomach and a lifeless marriage, is a sort of Swedish Everyman, and his assorted office colleagues also resemble a fair cross-section of the national psyche.

Walter Matthau starred as Beck, relocated and reimagined as a San Francisco cop, in the 1973 Stuart Rosenberg film. By this method the bare bones of the plot could be kept and the political complexities so integral to the basic Sjöwall-Wahlöö flavor eliminated. While the two communist authors deposited Hollywood capitalist cash into their bank accounts, the movie did draw memorable performances from the leads, in particular Bruce Dern as the villain.

47. · *Bank Shot*
by Donald E. Westlake · (1972)

*A*nother classic comic caper involving John Dortmunder and his gang of professional thieves for whom nothing ever seems to work precisely as masterminded.

Dortmunder has the perfect plan for robbing a bank. While the building is undergoing construction work, the bank is temporarily housed in a trailer. Why not simply tow it away and crack the safe at leisure, he suggests. *Seems* like a good idea . . .

Bank Shot was filmed in 1974, two years after its publication, in a not very successful feature starring George C. Scott and Joanna Cassidy.

48. · *The Third Man*
by Graham Greene · (1950)

*T*he Third Man, Greene's best-known work, was merely a short story, then a treatment for a movie published as a novella after the film was a successful release.

American novelist Rolo Martins comes to postwar Vienna to meet his friend Harry Lime and learns that he has been killed in a mysterious accident. When Martins sets out to learn what really happened, he becomes involved in a situation that imperils his own life.

Although listed as a favorite book, few have actually read *The Third Man,* the heart-stoppingly superb movie being much in the memory of most crime aficionados. Joseph Cotten, Alida Valli, and Orson Welles as Harry Lime were perfect in the film, which was written by Greene.

49. · *The Killer Inside Me*
by Jim Thompson · (1952)

*W*henever America's greatest *noir* writers are mentioned, Jim Thompson, after years of obscurity, is now ranked at the top. While tremendously successful in France, Thompson was relegated to writing paperbacks in the U.S., most of which quickly went out of print and were never reprinted in his lifetime. With the printing of this novel, and soon thereafter just about everything else he wrote, Thompson became the most overpraised writer of the 1980s, described as America's greatest crime writer by those who, presumably, had never read Chandler.

Told in the first person by Lou Ford, the sheriff of a small Texas town, this book is the chilling tale of a compulsive murderer who happens to be trusted and much liked by the people he is paid to protect.

Burt Kennedy directed the mediocre Warner Brothers film in 1976.

50. · *WHERE ARE THE CHILDREN?*
BY Mary Higgins Clark · (1975)

*M*ary Higgins Clark burst on to the national scene with this debut novel and began the cycle of contemporary supsense fiction featuring ordinary, usually suburban women forced to defend their innocence against charges of evildoing.

Nancy Harmon Eldredge, the embattled heroine of *Where are the Children?*, has begun a new life on Cape Cod, where she is raising two children with her second husband. But a malignant presence from her past is about to reappear and intends to convince the world, as he did once before, that Nancy is an infanticidal murderess.

A 1988 movie, featuring Barnard Hughes and Frederic Forrest, starred Jill Clayburg as the mother at the mercy of a deranged villain adept at playing the cat to her mouse.

51. · *"A" IS FOR ALIBI*
BY Sue Grafton · (1982)

*A*long with Sara Paretsky and Marcia Muller, Sue Grafton helped usher in the modern era of the female private eye. Her series character, Kinsey Millhone, is a twice-divorced Californian who is sleuthing her way through the alphabet (*"B"* Is for Burglar, *"C"* Is for Corpse, etc.). Hardworking and not afraid to get tough, Kinsey sets the standard for her fictional peers in terms of getting down to the frequently frustrating, usually unglamorous nitty-gritty of the job.

In *"A" Is for Alibi*, Kinsey is hired by a recent parolee, a still-young woman convicted of murdering her unfaithful husband eight years earlier. What Nikki Fife wants to do is prove her innocence. Reopening the case, however, means that the real killer is no longer safe and will be forced to strike again. This first mystery is also notable for the outcome of Kinsey's romantic involvement with one of the suspects.

52. · *THE FIRST DEADLY SIN*
BY Lawrence Sanders · (1973)

A suspense and mystery writer of great inventiveness, Lawrence Sanders is best known for *The Anderson Tapes* (1970), his debut work, and for his novels fitting into either the "Sins" or "Commandments" series. In *The First Deadly Sin* retired chief of detectives Edward X. Delaney, a secondary character in *The Anderson Tapes,* is reintroduced and given center stage. Nicknamed "Iron Balls," Delaney is a smoothly developed, highly likable protagonist whose appetite for unusual cases is as predictable as his appetite for mouthwatering sandwich combinations.

The First Deadly Sin pits Delaney against a psychotic serial killer at large in New York City. This memorable villain, calling himself AMROK II, imagines himself divinely inspired, committing brutal murders in order to enact God's will.

Frank Sinatra, starring in his first feature film in a decade, took top billing along with Faye Dunaway in the 1980 screen adaptation.

53. · *A THIEF OF TIME*
BY Tony Hillerman · (1988)

O nce again Tony Hillerman returns to the setting he has made completely his own, the Navajo reservations of the American Southwest, and once again he explores the conflicts experienced there as the desert's traditional guardians seek to maintain the spirit of the land against all odds.

Both Navajo Tribal Police officers Lt. Joe Leaphorn and Sgt. Jim Chee are featured in *A Thief of Time,* working together to discover the whereabouts of a missing anthropologist, last seen at an isolated excavation site.

The opening scene of this book, considered by many critics to be Hillerman's best, is a haunting one. It takes place on a moonlit night in a cliffside dwelling once occupied by an ancient people, the Anasazi, and comes to its chilling conclusion as the victim-to-be gets a glimpse of a mysterious pool and a frantic colony of tethered frogs. The phrase "thief of time" refers to unscrupulous pot-stealers who heedlessly plunder important artifacts from unprotected ruins.

54. · IN COLD BLOOD
BY Truman Capote · (1966)

*I*t is a major achievement for an author to turn a genre in a new direction; it is even more noteworthy for an author to create a new genre, which is exactly what Capote did with *In Cold Blood*. Called "faction" or "a true novel," it tells a true story in fictional form—creating dialogue, externalizing characters' thoughts, and so on. While it is a form that has been bastardized in recent years by lazy journalists and incompetent novelists, *In Cold Blood* remains a justly revered masterpiece.

On November 15, 1959, in a small Kansas town, four members of the Clutter family were brutally murdered by blasts from a shotgun held a few inches from their faces. There seemed to be no motive for the crimes, nor where there useful clues. On April 14, 1965, two men were hanged for the crime at the Kansas State Penitentiary. This book tells the stories of those six people.

Richard Brooks wrote and directed the atmospheric and faithful motion-picture version in 1967.

55. · ROGUE MALE
BY Geoffrey Household · (1939)

*T*he "what fun!" school of British mystery took a turn to the dark side with this psychological tale in which good sport unexpectedly devolves into nightmare. The death of innocence and the onset of World War II coincide, but not coincidentally.

A young British sportsman, bored with traditional game, takes a sporting challenge to stalk an unnamed European dictator (presumably Hitler). The goal is merely to get the dictator in the sights of his unloaded rifle. The sportsman is spotted, captured, tortured, and thrown over a cliff. Although he miraculously survives to return to England, he soon finds himself in peril again as German agents set out to finish the job.

Fritz Lang directed the excellent chase thriller retitled *Man Hunt* in 1941, starring Walter Pidgeon, Joan Bennett, and George Sanders.

56. · *MURDER MUST ADVERTISE*
BY Dorothy L. Sayers · (1933)

*D*rawing upon her own nine years' experience as an advertising copywriter at a London agency, Dorothy L. Sayers sets Lord Peter Wimsey to work at an honest job in the offices of Pym's Publicity. Calling himself Death Bredon (his two middle names), he is positioned to engage in a spot of undercover sleuthing while helping out on such accounts as Tom-Boy Toffee and Nutrax for Nerves.

Called in by the firm's head to investigate the suspicious death of an employee who'd tumbled fatally down the stairs at teatime, Wimsey takes gleefully to the task. He is, not surprisingly, a natural whiz at the clever absurdities of copywriting, but his pleasure in this newfound talent is punctuated by the occurrences of other not quite-accidental deaths.

This, the eighth Peter Wimsey novel, is Sayers's most overtly humorous performance. Aficionados, however, probably cherish it most for its repeated glimpses of Wimsey in harlequin costume, appearing and swiftly vanishing and then appearing again, as part of a seductive scheme to flush out a villain.

57. · THE INNOCENCE OF FATHER BROWN
BY G. K. Chesterton · (1911)

*T*here were no Father Brown novels, this being the first of five short-story collections and probably the best, since the puzzles and their solutions are first-rate. While the usual observation and deduction are integral parts of the stories, intuition plays a great role. Unlike the traditional detective story where a satisfying conclusion occurs when the criminal is caught and punished, the Father Brown stories are generally more likely to allow the thieves and other wrongdoers to remain free so that their souls may be saved.

Several film versions of "The Blue Cross," a short story from *The Innocence of Father Brown,* have been made, the first two starring Walter Connolly and Alec Guinness as the gentle priest.

58. · SMILEY'S PEOPLE
BY John le Carré · (1979)

*T*he final novel in the Smiley versus Karla trilogy, and indeed the final adventure of George Smiley (in which he quietly acknowledges that he won the epic battle against the Soviet superspy), *Smiley's People* is a rich, dense, slow, and beautiful work—a height to which le Carré has not risen again.

A former British secret agent (and former Soviet general) telephones British Intelligence with a message for Smiley. He once had worked for Smiley, been one of his people, but before he can speak to his now-retired supervisor, a Soviet-made assassination device speaks first, killing the defector. There is no choice but for Smiley to come out of his peaceful retirement and hunt down his nemesis.

Le Carré wrote the teleplay with John Hopkins for the PBS miniseries that starred Alec Guinness.

59. · *THE LADY IN THE LAKE*
BY Raymond Chandler · (1943)

*T*he fourth (of seven) Philip Marlowe novels is quintessential Chandler—the greatest of all American mystery writers—offering readers a first-rate plot, a wonderfully witty and intelligent writing style, and an unfailing sense of moral philosophy that helps to define the most distinguished literature.

A publisher hires the famous Los Angeles private detective to find his wife. When Marlowe finally locates her, it is at the bottom of a mountain lake.

A moderately successful film was made in 1946 with Robert Montgomery as Marlowe. While a standard private-eye movie in most respects, a gimmick was employed. The camera serves as the detective's eyes so that the audience can see only what Marlowe sees. The first glimpse of the detective occurs at the end of the film, when Marlowe sees his reflection in a mirror.

60. · *TO KILL A MOCKINGBIRD*
BY Harper Lee · (1960)

*P*art regional mystery, part timeless classic, *To Kill a Mockingbird* was universally acclaimed upon publication, making an instant celebrity of its publicity-shy author who never wrote another book of any kind. It won the Pulitzer Prize for fiction in 1961.

Narrated by Jean Louise "Scout" Finch, daughter of Atticus Finch, a small-town southern lawyer, the story looks back to a turbulent summer many years before, when Atticus's courageous defense of a black man wrongfully accused of rape ended in tragedy. Woven into the telling of the events leading up to the trial and its aftermath is the plight of Boo Radley, local recluse and favorite bogeyman to the neighborhood children. Both plot threads present lessons in tolerance that have long made this a classroom perennial.

The 1962 film adaptation won two Academy Awards: one for Gregory Peck's performance as Atticus Finch and one for Horton Foote's screenplay. It also marked the debut of actor Robert Duvall, who movingly created Boo Radley onscreen.

61. · *OUR MAN IN HAVANA*
BY Graham Greene · (1958)

*I*n one of his rare attempts at humor, Greene, a virulently anti-American communist, set his superb spoof in Cuba in the years just before Fidel Castro's reign.

A not-too-bright vacuum-cleaner salesman is recruited to be a British espionage agent in Havana by the head of Caribbean operations. Pressed for information, he sends elaborate plans for secret installations in the hills; actually, they are old designs for vacuum cleaners. He also sends fake reports and finds that they start to become frighteningly true.

Filmed in 1961 with Alec Guinness as Wormold, the ''spy,'' Greene closely based his screenplay on his novel.

62. · *THE MYSTERY OF EDWIN DROOD*
BY Charles Dickens · (1870)

*P*lanned by Dickens to be the greatest mystery novel ever written, perhaps because of his jealousy of the acclaim accorded to his friend Wilkie Collins's *The Moonstone,* this fascinating novel was never completed. After six (of a planned twenty) parts were written and published, Dickens died, leaving no notes or clues to his plans for the rest of the book.

Edwin Drood is engaged to Rosa Budd, but they do not love each other and decide to be just friends. She has returned the love of Ned Landless, seen walking with Drood the night he disappeared. Rosa's uncle and guardian, John Jasper, an opium addict who frightens Rosa by proclaiming his love for her, assures her that he has enough evidence to hang her lover. An obviously disguised mysterious stranger named Datchery arrives and sits at an open door, inexplicably making a white chalk mark every time Jasper's name is mentioned. Here the tale abruptly ends.

Drood was filmed in 1935 starring Claude Rains as Jasper and Heather Angel as Rosa. A successful Broadway musical, written by Rupert Holmes, had many different endings, each chosen by that night's audience.

63. · *WOBBLE TO DEATH*
BY Peter Lovesey · (1970)

A first-novel contest's sizable prize was the lure that convinced English schoolteacher Peter Lovesey to try his hand at crime writing. *Wobble to Death,* the result of his efforts, was acclaimed the winning entry. It introduced to readers the Victorian policemen Sergeant Cribb and Constable Thackeray, who went on to appear in seven further adventures. Such period settings as this, making use of little-known historical phenomena and detail, were uncommon a quarter-century ago and were thus all the more delightful for that reason.

Rather similar to the depression-era dance marathons, "wobbles" were sporting events that called for nonstop walking over a six-day duration. Against this unexpected background Lovesey devises a puzzle where a favorite competitor is murdered and Cribb and Thackeray are summoned to investigate. The suspense of learning who will win the race is—believe it or not—as intense as unmasking the murderer.

64. · *ASHENDEN*
BY W. Somerset Maugham · (1928)

*P*receded by Joseph Conrad's *The Secret Agent* (1907), *Ashenden* is incorrectly regarded as the first realistic spy novel. While Conrad's book had little influence on contemporary spy writers, Maugham's undoubtedly helped Graham Greene and Eric Ambler produce their nonheroic protagonists. The connected short stories in *Ashenden* feature a nonprofessional spy pressed into service and doing his best in difficult situations—the hallmark of most espionage fiction produced during the next quarter-century.

The central figure of *Ashenden* is a well-known author who is recruited as a secret agent by a British colonel known only as R to the Intelligence Department. His profession as a writer, it is reasoned, will allow him to travel without suspicion and give him access to people and places not always available to everyone.

One of the episodes in *Ashenden* served as the basis for Alfred Hitchcock's 1936 movie *The Secret Agent,* which starred Robert Young, Madeleine Carroll, John Gielgud, and Peter Lorre.

65. · *THE SEVEN PER-CENT SOLUTION*
BY Nicholas Meyer · (1974)

*T*his "newly discovered" manuscript of Dr. John H. Watson, in which a hitherto unknown adventure of Sherlock Holmes is recounted, was (deservedly) loathed by Sherlock Holmes aficionados immediately upon publication. The way in which Holmes is portrayed borders on sacrilege. The problem, of course, is that the book is wonderfully written, original, exciting, and went on to sell (deservedly) two million copies.

Holmes has gone to visit Sigmund Freud because of his cocaine-induced paranoia, which has taken such virulent hold that he believes oysters will overrun the earth and that a mild-mannered professor of mathematics named Moriarty is actually a diabolical genius, a spider at the center of the web of all crime in London.

Meyer adapted his own novel for the screen and was nominated for an Academy Award; the film was directed by Herbert Ross. Nicol Williamson played Holmes, Robert Duvall was Watson, and Alan Arkin portrayed Freud.

66. · *THE DOORBELL RANG*
BY Rex Stout (1965)

*I*n the annals of detective literature, perhaps only Sherlock Holmes and his supporting cast is more beloved than Nero Wolfe, the one-seventh-of-a-ton genius who relies on his tough assistant, Archie Goodwin, to do the legwork and other heavy lifting. The brownstone house on West 35th Street is nearly as familiar as the rooms at 221B Baker Street, and Fritz Brenner is clearly a more inspired cook than Mrs. Hudson. Wolfe even bears such a strong physical resemblance to Holmes's older brother, Mycroft, that it has been rumored that some genes were shared.

In *The Doorbell Rang* Wolfe agrees to take as a client a woman who claims she is being harassed by the FBI. Agents follow her, she says, and her telephones are tapped. Although Wolfe is hesitant to take the case, she offers him the largest retainer of his career and he soon finds himself in the midst of a murder investigation about which the FBI seems to know more than it is letting on.

Nero Wolfe has not been very well served in motion pictures, though Thayer David did a reasonable impersonation in the TV movie based on this novel.

67. · *STICK*
BY Elmore Leonard · (1983)

*Q*uite probably the best writer of dialogue in America, Leonard creates characters that *always* sound exactly right. As he pointed out when he was praised for the accuracy of the speech patterns among drug dealers in a Latino section of town, for example, he just writes the dialogue that he *thinks* would be spoken. The reader is unlikely to have spent much time on that street corner, and neither has Leonard. Still, there is a level of confidence that makes the speech cadences almost musical—and the music is jazz.

Stick is a wheeler-dealer in Florida, looking to make a buck on the Gold Coast. In this dangerous world of scams, sharks, double-dealers, killers, crooks (petty and very major), and mouthwatering fortunes, Stick finds the best deal of his life. Aided by a gorgeous blonde, he goes after a man who once tried to hurt him, aiming for sweet revenge and a sweet payday at the same time.

Burt Reynolds played the titular character in a movie that was not well received—especially by Leonard.

68. · THE LITTLE DRUMMER GIRL
BY John le Carré · (1983)

*A*lthough le Carré is best known for his novels about "The Circus," the British intelligence community, one of his bestselling titles is this thriller about the battle between a murderous Palestinian terrorist and an Israeli secret service officer.

Charlie, a beautiful actress, is set up as a sacrificial lamb when she insinuates herself into the life of the terrorists and learns the reality of deceit. As the action races from Bonn to London, Munich to Mykonos, Vienna to Jerusalem, the terrorist plots continue unabated while Kurtz, the Israeli leader, assembles his private army to bring them down. But the genuine hope of bringing the Palestinian to his end rests with Charlie, whose ambivalent commitment remains as complex and unresolved as the politics of the Middle East itself.

The Little Drummer Girl was filmed in 1984 with George Roy Hill directing and Diane Keaton in the eponymous role.

69. · *BRIGHTON ROCK*
BY Graham Greene · (1938)

*A*lthough Greene liked to separate his serious novels from his more popular fiction, which he called "entertainments," the distinction seems arbitrary at best, perhaps exemplified by *Brighton Rock,* which was published in England as a "novel" but in America as an "entertainment."

A teenage Catholic boy becomes the hardened leader of a tough gang. When a murder is committed on crowded Brighton Beach, a large, vulgar woman with a profound moral sense sets out to prove the killer is Pinkie, the violent boy of the slums who has married a devout, innocent sixteen-year-old girl to prevent her from testifying against him.

Brighton Rock was filmed in 1947 with Richard Attenborough.

70. · *DRACULA*
BY Bram Stoker · (1897)

*W*hile it stretches some definitions to call this Gothic horror story a mystery, it does employ several of the common elements of that classic form. Crimes of terrible violence are committed and a moral entity appears to discover the perpetrator, prevent further incidents, and bring the villain to a kind of justice. The fact that this particular villain uses supernatural means to accomplish his aims is what distinguishes this crime story from the traditional tale of mystery.

When Jonathan Harker visits the castle of Count Dracula, he quickly becomes a prisoner of his host, who sleeps in a coffin. Phantom women stalk the halls at night but disappear at dawn. Only when the count moves to London and is confronted by Dr. Van Helsing does Harker and his fiancée, Lucy, learn that they are being victimized by a vampire, a creature of extraordinary powers who is able to live for centuries by drinking the blood of his victims.

Frequently filmed, *Dracula* is among the handful of horror classics, the most memorable version starring Bela Lugosi, though the most accurate adaptation of the novel was filmed by Francis Coppola.

71. · *THE TALENTED MR. RIPLEY*
BY Patricia Highsmith · (1955)

*C*onsistently named as one of a half-dozen greatest of all suspense writers, Highsmith also created a truly unique character in Ripley, who has remained his totally amoral, if charming, self through five novels.

Ripley, a handsome young con artist, kills an American schoolmate while on a European holiday and assumes the identity of his wealthy friend.

After winning the Grand Prix de Littérature Policière as the best mystery translated into French in 1957, *The Talented Mr. Ripley* was filmed in France as *Purple Noon* and starred Alain Delon.

72. · *THE MOVING TOYSHOP*
BY Edmund Crispin · (1946)

*T*he witty and well-plotted mysteries of Crispin, the pseudonym of opera critic, musician, and composer Bruce Montgomery, have remained popular for a half-century, as their light-hearted charm is never weighed down by an overdose of erudition.

In one of the most baffling premises ever set forward in detective fiction, a poet discovers a corpse in a small room directly above a toy shop. He is knocked unconscious, and when he comes to, finds that the corpse is missing, but even more miraculously, so is the toy shop, which has been transformed into a grocery store.

73. · *A Time to Kill*
by John Grisham · (1989)

*O*riginally published to little notice, *A Time to Kill* became a paperback bestseller only after the release of Grisham's second novel, *The Firm,* made the author's name a household word.

Written in the spirit of *To Kill a Mockingbird,* it tells the story of Jake Brigance, a small-town Mississippi lawyer who decides to defend a black man, Carl Lee Hailey, against the charge of murdering two whites. The problem is that Carl Lee committed his crime in full view of the local citizenry, avenging himself definitively on the pair of redneck thugs who had viciously raped and beaten his fragile ten-year-old daughter.

Alcohol and idealism equally fuel Carl Lee's defense team, which, besides Jake, is composed of Lucien Wilbanks, local aristocrat and legendary legal maverick, and Ellen Roark, a tough-talking Yankee volunteer. The formula of underdog versus establishment is tackled by Grisham as if he were reinventing the wheel, and he nearly does.

74. · *Last Seen Wearing*
by Hillary Waugh · (1952)

*A*lthough the greatest and most famous American writer of police procedurals is Ed McBain, the form was created in the 1940s and early 1950s by Lawrence Treat and Hillary Waugh. Instead of private eyes or amateur sleuths, or even colorful policemen working solo, the police procedural carefully details, in a more or less realistic manner, the details of a criminal investigation as it would occur in real life, with real cops and credible methodology depicted.

In Waugh's finest work, the disappearance of a college girl in Massachusetts spurs a missing-persons search that requires all the skill that the local police can provide.

The author was presented with a Grand Master Award by the Mystery Writers of America in 1988 for lifetime achievement.

75. · LITTLE CAESAR
BY W. R. Burnett · (1929)

*T*he first important book about gangsters, published while Prohibition and the Chicago gang wars raged, *Little Caesar* became the prototype for all subsequent crime novels set in that milieu. Told from a gangster's point of view, this story of a hoodlum's rise and fall remains one of the most important crime novels ever written.

When the vicious Cesare Bandello—known as Rico, or Little Caesar—kills a cop during a holdup, he acquires the confidence and power to challenge his boss for the leadership of their gang— his first big step up the ladder of power and wealth in the Chicago underworld. When one of the gang rats on him, however, Rico must flee, quickly betraying himself as a bully and a coward.

The famous 1930 film version catapulted Edward G. Robinson to fame as the ultimate screen hoodlum and became the model for most successful gangster movies.

76. · THE FRIENDS OF EDDIE COYLE
BY George V. Higgins · (1972)

*I*nstantly proclaimed one of the genre's most distinctive voices, George V. Higgins might also be termed the Damon Runyon of the Massachusetts bar. His portrayals of petty hoods and urban pols on the take, richly flavored with the idiom of the Boston Irish as he hears and then reinvents it, are important additions to the literature of the law. Higgins, himself an attorney, has a fine eye for crime's comedy.

In *The Friends of Eddie Coyle* Eddie's problem is that while he has visions of a big score, the deal he's trying to make keeps turning into a deal he's unable to control. A small-timer, he hustles himself past the point of no return in a setup where guns and money prove their usual lethal mix.

Peter Yates directed Robert Mitchum and Peter Boyle in the 1973 screen version.

77. · *CLOUDS OF WITNESS*
BY Dorothy L. Sayers · (1927)

*T*he second Peter Wimsey novel, *Clouds of Witness,* takes as its starting point a remarkable supposition: that Lord Peter's brother, Gerald, the sixteenth Duke of Denver, is a murderer. Or at least that's the finding of the coroner's jury after a houseguest at Riddlesdale Lodge has been found shot and the weapon identified as the duke's own army revolver. Yet despite its challenging puzzle, *Clouds of Witness* is more than anything anthropological, with its glimpses into the peculiar codes governing the lives of the British nobility.

With regard to the untimely death of Capt. Denis Cathcart, the duke actually had the motive as well as the opportunity. He had quarreled with the man, soon to be his brother-in-law, after hearing the charge that Cathcart had once earned his living in Paris cheating at cards. Such caddish behavior could not be tolerated in a man to whom Denver would give his sister in marriage.

Sayers studiously explores every possible angle to the duke's apparent guilt. But the real difficulty, as Lord Peter, sleuthing against his brother's express wishes, eventually learns, is that Denver is guilty. Quite, quite guilty, in fact. Only his crime is not the one of which he stands accused.

78. · *FROM RUSSIA, WITH LOVE*
BY Ian Fleming · (1957)

*C*ombining the most romantic elements of the old-fashioned spy story with the strength of the American hard-boiled private-eye novel, Fleming's James Bond is one of the most popular crime-fighting figures of the twentieth century.

The dashing Bond takes on the enormously powerful international criminal organization, SPECTRE, which is interested in world domination because of the wealth that would accrue. It is a menace both to the West and the usual Bond adversary, the Soviet Union.

From Russia, with Love is the second in the series of James Bond movies, starring Sean Connery, that proved to be the most successful sequence of films in the 1960s. Beginning with *Dr. No* in 1963 and followed by *Goldfinger, Thunderball,* and *You Only Live Twice,* the tongue-in-cheek adventures all featured supervillains, beautiful girls, and delightfully inventive weaponry.

79. · *BEAST IN VIEW*
BY Margaret Millar · (1955)

*A*s the wife of Ross Macdonald (Kenneth Millar), Margaret Millar staked out fictional territory very different from that of her husband. Prefiguring such writers as Patricia Highsmith and Ruth Rendell, she made her lasting reputation with novels of twisted psyches on a collision course with disaster.

Beast in View offers a portrait of a wealthy spinster who begins to complain of persecution at the hands of a peculiar former acquaintance, a young woman at once violent and sly.

Winner of the Edgar Allan Poe Award for best novel, *Beast in View* is a skillful early handling of multiple personality disorder in the contemporary mystery.

80. · *SMALLBONE DECEASED*
BY Michael Gilbert · (1950)

*A*lthough a successful mystery writer and recipient of the Grand Master Award by the Mystery Writers of America, Gilbert has remained a solicitor since 1947. For many years his best-known client was Raymond Chandler. Virtually all his novels and short stories have been written in longhand during his train commute between Kent and London.

Like many others of his works, *Smallbone Deceased* is set in a lawyer's office. This droll, slightly satiric novel explores the problems that arise when a body is discovered in a safe-deposit box.

81. · *THE FRANCHISE AFFAIR*
BY Josephine Tey · (1948)

*T*ey's series detective, Alan Grant, makes only a brief appearance in this retelling of the famous eighteenth-century Elizabeth Canning case.

A young lawyer with a comfortable civil practice is suddenly asked to defend two women, a mother and a daughter, who have been accused by a teenage girl of imprisoning her and abusing her over a period of two weeks.

A low-budget film version, starring Michael Denison, Dulcie Gray, and Anthony Nicholls, was released in 1951.

82. · *CROCODILE ON THE SANDBANK*
BY Elizabeth Peters · (1975)

*A*fter graduating with a degree in Egyptology, the author had no intention of using that rather arcane knowledge in a detective story, but circumstances allowed it and her most popular (of several) series of mystery stories features Amelia Peabody, a young archaeologist with a special interest in Egypt—an unusual profession in the Victorian era.

Having inherited her father's fortune (and his strong will), Amelia heads to Cairo to indulge her interest in Egyptology. On the way she befriends Evelyn Barton-Forbes, who accompanies her to Egypt and is promptly attacked by a homicidal mummy. Amelia enlists the aid of Radcliffe Emerson to unravel the inexplicable threats of the mummy, who seems intent on murdering them all.

83. · *SHROUD FOR A NIGHTINGALE*
BY P. D. James · (1971)

*O*ne of the most acclaimed of all contemporary mystery writers, P. D. James has struggled, to some degree successfully, to be seen as a novelist unconfined by genre designations. Yet when she is recognized as the "queen of crime," it is only because her career has brought her a level of fame nearly unseen for a woman in the genre since the days of Christie and Sayers.

In this, her fourth novel, James draws upon her own experiences as a Red Cross nurse during the Second World War. It is set in a nursing hospital outside of London where Inspector Adam Dalgliesh of Scotland Yard, her series detective, has been called in to investigate the murder of a student nurse poisoned in full view of her peers while helping to demonstrate a routine medical procedure.

As is always the case with James, the plot is mostly concerned with relationships and with human character. And as is usually the case with a mystery set in such a closed community, with a cast of fixed suspects, nearly every person Dalgliesh encounters is concealing a guilty secret.

84. · *THE HUNT FOR RED OCTOBER*
BY Tom Clancy · (1984)

*W*hen John F. Kennedy publicly stated that he admired Ian Fleming's James Bond stories, they immediately shot onto the bestseller lists, just as a quiet English writer named J. S. Fletcher became an overnight success when Woodrow Wilson mentioned that he thought *The Middle Temple Murders* was a worthwhile read. The same lightning hit Clancy when Ronald Reagan spoke of his pleasure in reading *The Hunt for Red October,* the first work of fiction by the normally academic Naval Institute Press. Its description as a techno-thriller added a new phrase to the language.

Under the Atlantic, Capt. Marko Ramius of the Soviet missile submarine *Red October* has made the greatest decision of his life, and perhaps of the entire Cold War. He has decided to head toward America. Is he, without orders, launching an attack? Or is he defecting with the top-secret sub?

An exciting film version of the book was released in 1990, starring Sean Connery and Alec Baldwin.

85. · *CHINAMAN'S CHANCE*
BY Ross Thomas · (1978)

*O*ne of the secret giants of crime fiction in America has been for many years Ross Thomas, whose inventiveness and intelligence are unsurpassed by any living writer. Cognoscenti have fruitlessly argued about which of Thomas's many funny, cynical, exquisitely peopled novels is the best. This one is as good a choice as any, though his Edgar winners, *The Cold War Swap* and *Briarpatch* are also wonderful, as are *The Fools in Town Are on Our Side* and *The Seersucker Whipsaw* and *Out on the Rim* and *Missionary Stew* and . . . well, all of them.

Artie Wu, the thirty-seven-year-old pretender to the throne of China, and his partner, Quincy Durant, are a couple of con men with a lot of experience and a lot of the right friends. Among the large cast of characters are a multimillionaire, a missing woman, and a Mafia boss and his former college roommate, who had once been in the CIA. A lot of money is at stake, but no one seems to know who is planning to do what to whom.

86. · *THE SECRET AGENT*
BY Joseph Conrad · (1907)

*O*ften regarded as the first serious novel to feature an espionage agent, *The Secret Agent* was largely based on an actual historical incident.

Verloc becomes involved with anarchists who continue a complex and heinous plot to commit a shocking crime of violence on an unsuspecting group of innocent people in London's Greenwich Park.

Alfred Hitchcock filmed *The Secret Agent* in 1936 as *Sabotage* (U.S. title: *The Woman Alone*) starring Sylvia Sidney and Oscar Homolka.

87. · *THE DREADFUL YELLOW SKY*
BY John D. MacDonald · (1975)

*O*ne of the best-loved storytellers of the twentieth century, John D. MacDonald was a prolific pulp writer (once writing all of the stories in a magazine using a different pseudonym for each) and then a prolific paperback and hardcover author. His greatest creation was Travis McGee, the handsome adventurer who lived on his houseboat, *The Busted Flush,* in Ft. Lauderdale.

A rugged boat bum, part philosopher, part detective, part crook, McGee agrees to do a favor for a former girlfriend. Hide a hundred thousand dollars for her, she asks, with no questions asked. He agrees, but learns a few days later that she is dead. When he investigates her past, McGee becomes embroiled with drug smugglers, crooked politicians, and a bunch of gorgeous swinging singles.

88. · *THE GLASS KEY*
BY Dashiell Hammett · (1931)

*P*robably the finest of Hammett's five novels in terms of plot structure, subtlety, and depth of characterization, this tale of political corruption and its ambient notions of friendship and loyalty was Hammett's personal favorite of all his work.

Freelance political troubleshooter Ned Beaumont remains loyal to his boss, Paul Madvig, a totally corrupt political boss. When Beaumont falls in love with Madvig's daughter, the men's relationship is strained by the politico's desire for his daughter to marry someone higher on the social ladder. Beaumont appears to have been based largely on Hammett himself: both were tall, slim, mustachioed, heavy drinkers, gamblers, sufferers from tuberculosis, cynical, but loyal to friends and ideals.

The Glass Key was well filmed twice, once in 1935 with George Raft as Beaumont, Edward Arnold as Madvig, and Claire Todd as his daughter; and again in 1942 with Alan Ladd, Brian Donlevy, and Veronica Lake.

89. · *JUDGMENT IN STONE*
BY Ruth Rendell · (1977)

A peerless creator of mood and menace, Ruth Rendell coolly, slowly, and with painstaking attention to human short circuits dispatches her characters to their assorted fates. Her nonseries novels—the ones that do not feature Inspector Wexford of the Kingsmarkham force—such as *Judgment in Stone,* all treat the potential for chaos and destruction that lies and waits in the aberrant psyche. Her worst villains often look to be the least likely agents of doom.

In *Judgment in Stone* the tragedy is set in motion when one of Eunice Parchman's blackmail victims decides to read aloud to her a help wanted ad placed by a rural family seeking a housekeeper. For all of Eunice's shrewdness, which enables her to extort small sums of money from erring neighbors, she fights hardest to keep her own secret. Unfortunately, this secret, combined with her repressed, resentful nature, makes Eunice a lethal presence in the unsuspecting Coverdale household.

90. · *BRAT FARRAR*
BY Josephine Tey · (1950)

A great favorite of intellectuals who read mysteries but feel compelled to explain their evident dysfunction, Tey lives up to the praise heaped upon her. Under a different publishing plan this novel might be described as a romance, though it certainly has its share of criminal tension.

Simon Ashby, soon to turn twenty-one, will inherit his mother's fortune. All that stands in the way is Brat Farrar, who resembled Simon's twin brother, Patrick, believed drowned some years earlier. Farrar has Patrick's mannerisms and seems to know every detail of his life. But when Simon learns that Farrar is an impostor, out to cheat him of his inheritance, he fails to expose him. Why?

Two television specials have been based on *Brat Farrar,* neither one of great distinction.

91. · *THE CHILL*
BY Ross Macdonald · (1963)

W hen the great hard-boiled writers are listed, the pantheon is generally restricted to the Big Three: Hammett, Chandler, and Macdonald. Consciously emulating the style of Chandler, Macdonald's early works were excellent pastiches, but it is with

The Chill that he found his own voice—the voice that would prove to influence an entire generation of crime writers.

Lew Archer, the quintessential California private eye, takes the case of a missing bride that soon becomes a nasty murder investigation when she turns up in a pool of blood. As with virtually all of Archer's cases, the roots of the crime are imbedded in the past.

Paul Newman played Archer twice, changing the name to Harper (apparently for superstitious reasons) in both.

92. · *Devil in a Blue Dress*
BY Walter Mosley · (1990)

Already one of the hottest writers of the early 1990s, Mosley's career got a boost when President Clinton announced that Mosley was his favorite mystery writer. One of the flew black authors in the history of crime fiction, Mosley brought a new place and new sensibility to vast numbers of readers.

Easy Rawlins is a black war veteran in 1948 Los Angeles. He has just lost his job in a defense plant and is drinking at a local bar, trying to figure out what to do next, when a white man in a white suit approaches him and asks him to find a sexy blond beauty, Daphne Monet, who is known to frequent black jazz clubs. He agrees, and decides that being a private eye may be dangerous but sometimes so is crossing the street.

Devil in a Blue Dress was nominated for an Edgar Allan Poe Award for the best first mystery of the year

93. · *The Choirboys*
BY Joseph Wambaugh · (1975)

One of the most influential crime writers of the past quarter-century, Wambaugh is responsible for the modern police novel. A Los Angeles policeman for twenty years, he brought a new sensibility and realism to stories about cops, filling his novels with anecdotes and people that remain in the reader's consciousness long after the book is done. Mood swings are abrupt in his episodic narratives, racing from hilarity to tragedy and back to joy in moments.

Ten cops who work on nightwatch are dubbed "the choirboys" as they meet after work in Los Angeles's MacArthur Park to drink, talk, laugh, cry, have sex, and generally raise hell.

Robert Aldrich directed a raucous screen version in 1977 with many recognizable and talented actors as the choirboys: Charles Durning, James Woods, Don Stroud, Randy Quaid, Burt Young, Charles Haid, and Lou Gossett, Jr., among others.

94. · GOD SAVE THE MARK
BY Donald E. Westlake · (1967)

*T*he author won the Edgar Allan Poe Award from the Mystery Writers of America for the Best Novel of 1967 with this achingly funny adventure. It is the story of the ultimate patsy, the poor jerk who falls for every scam and con artist who even *thinks* about duping him. When he is the unexpected recipient of several hundred thousand dollars, the wise guys line up to get a piece of it. At *least* a piece of it.

Westlake, the ultimate comic mystery writer, went on to receive more Edgars and nominations in more categories than any other author, which culminated in a Grand Master Award for lifetime achievement in 1993.

95. · HOME SWEET HOMICIDE
BY Craig Rice · (1944)

*I*t is stretching a point to state that this is an autobiographical novel, but there is no question that the author, whose real name was Georgiana Ann Randolph, incorporated much of her own life as a mystery writer in this novel, which was published at the height of the "isn't murder fun?" period of mystery fiction.

A young widow with three children supports them all by writing mysteries. When her offspring hear gunshots from a nearby house, she inevitably becomes involved in a murder case. She also becomes involved, equally inevitably, with the handsome bachelor police detective assigned to the case.

Home Sweet Homicide was filmed in 1946 and starred Lynn Bari, Randolph Scott, James Gleason, and Peggy Ann Garner.

96. · *THE THREE COFFINS*
BY John Dickson Carr · (1935)

*T*he greatest of all creators of the locked-room puzzle or the "impossible" crime, Carr offered the most extraordinary episode of pure arrogant showing-off when he had his detective, Dr. Gideon Fell, deliver a lecture in which he divulged scores of tricks, illusions, and devices that could have been used to commit this murder. Of course, none was the true solution of this tour de force.

Two people saw a masked figure enter Professor Grimaud's study. They heard a shot. When the police arrived and broke down the locked door, there was no sign of the masked killer. Outside the window the fresh snow was pristine, with no hint of footprints. A careful examination showed no secret doors or hiding places. Only the keen eye and nimble brain of Dr. Fell stands between the murderer and success.

97. · *PRIZZI'S HONOR*
BY Richard Condon · (1982)

*O*ne of the most inventive American thriller writers, Richard Condon sustains a level of sophistication and cynicism so high it's actually easy to understand why his isn't a household name. Yet some of his novels, most notably *The Manchurian Candidate* (1959), might qualify for that description. *Prizzi's Honor* began a fresh cycle in the erratic Condon career, which has been an American life with a second inning, perhaps because he has consistently found new ways to exploit paranoia.

In the case of the Prizzi family, he takes on both the mob and the nature of true love, making the former seem far less lethal than the latter. Since one of the major characters is a ruthless hit woman, it's safe to say that Condon simply never wishes his readers to feel safe—that he'd rather leave them squirming.

The 1985 screen version, with a script co-authored by Condon, was directed by John Huston and featured an Academy Award–winning performance by Anjelica Huston. Jack Nicholson and Kathleen Turner also starred, turning in equally unforgettable performances as the slow-witted Mafia contract guy and the dubious dame he falls for.

98. · *THE STEAM PIG*
BY James McClure · (1974)

*W*ith books set in apartheid South Africa, it would be simplicity itself for McClure to get on a soapbox and lecture readers about the inequities of the system. Instead he tells straightforward and beautifully written police procedurals about two cops who work together on a daily basis: Lt. Tromp Kramer, an Afrikaaner, and his Zulu assistant, Sgt. Zondi. Their relationship, and the people who interact with them, are portrayed with a depth of understanding that is absent from the political tracts that purport to deal more intellectually with the subject.

At a funeral parlor in Trekkersburg, a pleasant and peaceful small town, two bodies are awaiting disposal. By a fluke accident they are switched, and the body of a respectable young music teacher, whose death was diagnosed as a straightforward case of heart failure, is sent for an autopsy, where doctors discover that she was murdered by a nearly invisible wound from a bicycle spoke—a murder method peculiar to certain Bantu gangsters. The police must discover what possible link there could be between a young white woman and Bantus, especially in a town where blacks and whites are strictly separated.

The Steam Pig, the author's first novel, won the British Gold Dagger Award as the best mystery of the year.

99. · *TIME AND AGAIN*
BY Jack Finney · (1970)

*T*ime and Again is one of those rarities: a universally loved book. More fantasy than mystery, it nonetheless offers various elements of criminal behavior, although the interest these present to the reader is overshadowed by the wondrous time-travel effects. Claimed as a mystery writer but always with caveats, Jack Finney—whose works include two other, very dissimilar, classics, *Assault on a Queen* (1959) and *The Body Snatchers* (1955)—can equally be considered a member in high standing of the science fiction, fantasy, or horror communities. The truth, though, is that he simply has followed his imagination wherever it has led him.

Si Morley, the artist hero of *Time and Again,* is invited to become a participant in a secret government program that is attempting to send suitable subjects back into actual eras of American history, from where they will be able to return with eyewitness reports. Said project's purposes may be too innocuous to be true, but the opportunity to become a temporary citizen of 1880s New York City is more tantalizing than Si can resist. However, as the truth of what he's involved with begins to dawn on him, he is resourceful enough to turn the tables on his handlers. The result is a rousingly romantic adventure yarn that holds up to regular rereadings.

100. · A MORBID TASTE FOR BONES
BY Ellis Peters · (1977)

Although Ellis Peters won the Edgar Allan Poe Award for best mystery of the year in 1963 for a novel about Inspector Felse, *Death and the Joyful Woman,* she is best known for her excellent and authentic series about Brother Cadfael, a monk in the twelfth-century Benedictine monastery of Shrewsbury.

When the ambitious prior of the monastery learns of the existence of the bones of an obscure saint who nonetheless was reputed to have magical powers, he forms a party to travel to the small Welsh town in which they rest. The relics, he believes, will bring prestige to his monastery. The prior and his party encounter numerous obstacles, including murder and a surfeit of unwanted miracles. It remains for the gentle herbalist, Cadfael, to sort out the bones and the bodies.

A British television series, which premiered in the fall of 1993, was devoted to life in a medieval monastery as seen through the eyes of the monk who came late to the religious life.

101. · ROSEMARY'S BABY
BY Ira Levin · (1967)

The author of this classic novel of terror admits to some guilt for helping to spawn the revival of supernatural thrillers with the enormous success of this story, both as a novel and as a film. Very little success had come to tales of witches and demons, exorcisms and omens in the years prior to *Rosemary's Baby,* and a great deal has come to them since. While not a mystery novel in the classic sense, it certainly has more than its share of suspense, crime, evil, and shocking twists. It is, nonetheless, astonishing to find it on the list of the 100 best mysteries when Levin's brilliant first novel, *A Kiss Before Dying,* failed to find a spot.

Guy and Rosemary Woodhouse are newlyweds who move into the Bramford, an apartment house (based on New York's legendary Dakota) with a strange history. Guy grows increasingly friendly with some of the eccentric tenants, but when Rosemary becomes pregnant, the interest of their neighbors becomes more and more ominous.

Roman Polanski's superb film version was exceptionally faithful to the novel and has become a classic in its own right. Mia Farrow played the titular mother and John Cassavetes was Guy.

These Writers Received a Significant Number of Votes

But No Single Title Predominated

❧

Margery Allingham

Lawrence Block

Simon Brett

James Lee Burke

James Ellroy

Dick Francis

Martha Grimes

Helen MacInnes

Ngaio Marsh

Sara Paretsky

Robert B. Parker

Ellery Queen

Georges Simenon

Cornell Woolrich

Favorite Female Writer
1. Agatha Christie
2. Dorothy Sayers
3. Sue Grafton

Favorite Male Writer
1. Raymond Chandler
2. Tony Hillerman
3. Arthur Conan Doyle

Favorite Female Sleuth
1. Miss Marple
2. Kinsey Millhone
3. V. I. Warshawski

Favorite Male Sleuth
1. Philip Marlowe
2. Sherlock Holmes
3. Lord Peter Wimsey

Favorite Cities for Murder
1. NEW YORK: The New York cited is Nero Wolfe's New York in the Rex Stout books, the New York of *Cat of Many Tails* by Ellery Queen, and the New York of Lawrence Block. Also mentioned for their New York settings were books by Cornell Woolrich, Lillian O'Donnell, and Stanley Ellin.
2. LONDON: The London is overwhelmingly the London of Sherlock Holmes, with prominent mention also given to the London of Margery Allingham's *The Tiger in the Smoke,* as well as the London of Dorothy L. Sayers and Christie's Hercule Poirot.
3. LOS ANGELES: Raymond Chandler's Los Angeles predominates, but it is also the Los Angeles of Jonathan Kellerman and James M. Cain's *Double Indemnity.*
   ALSO MENTIONED: The San Francisco of *The Maltese Falcon,* the Chicago of Sara Paretsky and Fredric Brown, and Maigret's Paris.

Favorite Murder Weapon

1. A frozen leg of lamb, later served for dinner, in Roald Dahl's short story "Lamb to the Slaughter."
2. A snake. The snake is used as a murder weapon in both Conan Doyle's "The Speckled Band" and Rex Stout's *Fer-de-lance*. These two works received an equal number of votes, to put the snake in second place.
3. The church bells in Dorothy L. Sayers's *The Nine Tailors*.

Favorite Hiding Place for a Body

1. The window seat in *Arsenic and Old Lace*.
2. The stomach, as in consuming it, in Lord Dunsany's "Two Bottles of Relish" and Stanley Ellin's "Specialty of the House."
3. A bale of wool, in *Died in the Wool,* by Ngaio Marsh.

Favorite Animal in a Mystery Novel

1. The hound in *The Hound of the Baskervilles*.
2. Asta in *The Thin Man*.
3. The Siamese cats in *The Cat Who . . .* series by Lilian Jackson Braun.

Favorite Mystery Movie

1. *The Maltese Falcon* (more than doubled any other)
2. *Chinatown*
3. *Silence of the Lambs*
   Also popular: *Body Heat, Laura, The Lady Vanishes, Psycho, Rear Window,* and *The Third Man*

Part Two

THE TOP TEN BOOKS BY CATEGORY

Classics

---

1 · *THE COMPLETE SHERLOCK HOLMES,* Arthur Conan Doyle
  Including these individual high vote-getters:
  THE HOUND OF THE BASKERVILLES
  A STUDY IN SCARLET
  THE ADVENTURES OF SHERLOCK HOLMES
  THE SIGN OF FOUR

2 · *TALES OF MYSTERY AND IMAGINATION,* Edgar Allan Poe
  Including this individual high vote-getter:
  "THE MURDERS IN THE RUE MORGUE"

3 · *THE MOONSTONE,* Wilkie Collins

4 · *THE WOMAN IN WHITE,* Wilkie Collins

5 · *CRIME AND PUNISHMENT,* Fyodor Dostoevski

6 · *TRENT'S LAST CASE,* E. C. Bentley

7 · *THE CIRCULAR STAIRCASE,* Mary Roberts Rinehart

8 · *THE MYSTERY OF EDWIN DROOD,* Charles Dickens

9 · *THE INNOCENCE OF FATHER BROWN,* G. K. Chesterton

10 · *DRACULA,* Bram Stoker

The Classical Genre

━♦━

BY H. R. F. KEATING

*W*hen you look at the immense panorama of mystery fiction today, encompassing a criminous version of almost every sort of novel there has ever been, it is extraordinary to think that it all sprang from three short stories written for magazines between 1841 and 1845 when Edgar Allan Poe collected them, with a lot of his other writings, in *Tales of Mystery and Imagination.* But with those three accounts of how Le Chevalier C. Auguste Dupin solved three mysterious crimes Poe laid down once and forever the rules and foundation for a new sort of fiction. Fiction that has proliferated and proliferated to fill shelf after shelf in bookstore and library, column after column in the review pages.

Of course, that sweeping statement, like all sweeping statements, is not wholly true. Certainly Poe's example was followed. But not immediately and not exclusively. When, some forty years after Poe's stories, mystery fiction took on its great popularity it swept up in its wake a whole lot of rubbish and a few discarded precious stones. I use the word *rubbish* advisedly since much of what got incorporated into pure detective fiction might well be called just that. It incorporated sensational stories of every kind, ghastly murders, horrid robberies, mustachioed villains looming over innocent maidens (mostly wearing white muslin nightdresses), any blood-and-thunderosities you care to think of. They gave our art bulk but mercifully never quite swamped the true original thread.

It was this thread, first spun by Poe, that was given length and breadth and strength in the years after 1887, with Arthur Conan Doyle's accounts of the adventures of Sherlock Holmes, stories that rightly, I think, top the list of choices made in the classical genre by members of the Mystery Writers of America. If Poe, in a lightning stroke of genius, created the Great Detective, the key figure of mystery writing, Doyle, took the puling infant and, in the words of Charles Dickens, "brought it up by hand."

Dupin was conceived as a pattern hero for that immense up-heaval in Western thought that goes by the name of the Romantic Revolution. He was to be, and was, a prototype of the human being who believed that the rules of existence sprang, not from any long-laid-down precepts of the ancient masters, but from each individ-ual's own concept of what life should be. He was the detective as model, the story hero who showed all readers how to break out of the prisons of their preconceptions.

But Dupin was a model, the carved statue of the Great Detec-tive. Doyle made the statue flesh. In Sherlock Holmes he gave us a man with whom, despite the tremendous intellectual powers he was endowed with, we can identify. Holmes, with his endearing weaknesses, the recourse to mind-affecting substances, his ready-to-be-pricked pride, is someone we can believe in as a real person. Witness the letters that still arrive today at the London office block at 221B Baker Street begging for his help.

It was because of the enormous success of the short stories about Holmes, as they appeared in the *Strand Magazine* in England and in the United States in *Harper's Weekly* and *Colliers* that there followed imitations of every sort. Then came the parodies and pas-tiches that many of us still delight in producing even today. But, more important, there were the crime solvers in the Sherlock mold plus the anti-Holmes detectives, above all G. K. Chesterton's un-scientific, religion-permeated Father Brown, ninth in the list of classical choices.

After Poe, then, the chain can be seen linking on one from another, first Holmes, then Father Brown, then such now forgotten figures as Ernest Bramah's blind detective Max Carrados and on to Agatha Christie's Hercule Poirot, Dorothy L. Sayers's Lord Peter Wimsey, Ellery Queen's Ellery Queen, Rex Stout's Nero Wolfe, variation after variation. But at the same time there was the mis-cellaneous rubbish of sensational literature (Watson remarked on Holmes's immense knowledge of it) that stuck like so many bar-nacles to the chain's iron links. The rubbish and the jewels that lay among the rubbish.

Foremost of those jewels are the two Wilkie Collins novels

that were the third and fourth choices of the busily listing MWA members, *The Moonstone* and *The Woman in White*. The former, in fact, headed the roll call of writers' favorites among the classics when the Crime Writers' Association in Britain took a similar poll in 1990. Nor would I say our choice was wrong. Almost any praise you care to bestow on *The Moonstone* can be justified, even, bar some minor inaccuracy, T. S. Eliot's "the first, the longest and the best of modern English detective stories."

It contains countless things that writers in our field have since seized on. It is a perfect example of the story of the innocent man who, with every circumstance against him, must be proved guiltless after all. Its detective, the marvelously drawn Sergeant Cuff, actually pronounces those words, used by so many of us since, "the pieces of the puzzle are not all put together." And he couples them with "I have never met with such a thing as a trifle yet" (Sir Arthur Conan Doyle, please copy). He even speaks of "the dirtiest ways of this dirty little world," an expression that would come very nicely from the lips of Dashiell Hammett's Sam Spade. And, note, that archetypal rejection of the British detective story's manor house for urban California's mean streets begins with a whopping clue in the best classical murder-mystery vein.

But *The Moonstone* is something more than a mystery, as are half the other top ten in our list: *The Woman in White,* Dostoevski's *Crime and Punishment,* Bram Stoker's pure horror tale *Dracula,* Mary Roberts Rinehart's *The Circular Staircase* (Why does that old house have a *circular* staircase? Answer: Because it is a powerful symbol), and, for all its guess-what element, Dickens's *The Mystery of Edwin Drood.* These are pure novels with a mystery tug rather than true crime fiction. The difference, as I see it, is that the pure novel is written because its author wants above all to tell his readers, or hers, what the world is like, while mystery fiction is written primarily to entertain its readers and has as a secondary aim only the object of saying, to as large an extent as the need to hold the reader will allow, what is the way things are.

So would a stern surveyor from the other side of the Atlantic (but as an MWA member I had my vote) rule out all those chosen peaks of the art from this list? No, I think, despite the very different purpose Dostoevski, for instance, had when he told of the terrible mind-adventures of the student Raskolnikov, these books can be placed among the exemplars all mystery writers after them can look up to.

Because, whatever was the way of it from the 1920s to the 1940s, nowadays there is in almost all mystery fiction a large element of the pure novel. In 1913 there was no alternative for a writer filled with doubt about the artificiality of the detective story, like E. C. Bentley, but to attempt a put-down of it on its own terms. The fact that *Trent's Last Case* turned out to be as good a classic of the detective genre as any is only a fine piece of irony.

But now there are other ways open to the writer who while acknowledging the foundations of the detective story wants to do more than it ever could. For better or worse we mystery writers today make even bigger claims on the straight novelists' territory. We are almost all at it, whether blatantly knocking at the reader's front door, like the feminist mystery writers who force open our male eyes so delightfully, or whether by subtly slipping in at an unlatched window with stories that have some hardly visible underlying theme.

So we can gain inspiration from these forebears. Be it from *The Moonstone* with its symbolism of the Shivering Sands, that seemingly tranquil surface beneath which lie the terrors of the irrational. Be it from the half-hidden sexuality of *The Woman in White*. Or from that great study of evil *Crime and Punishment*. Or from that study of the duality of our human nature *The Mystery of Edwin Drood,* so much more than a mere mystery of a murderer to be named. The classics of our earliest days still speak to us in no small voices.

Suspense

———— ✦✦ ————

1 · *REBECCA*, Daphne du Maurier
2 · *THE SILENCE OF THE LAMBS*, Thomas Harris
3 · *RED DRAGON*, Thomas Harris
4 · *WHERE ARE THE CHILDREN?* Mary Higgins Clark
5 · *LAURA*, Vera Caspary
6 · *BEAST IN VIEW*, Margaret Millar
7 · *JUDGMENT IN STONE*, Ruth Rendell
8 · *ROSEMARY'S BABY*, Ira Levin
9 · *THE BIG CLOCK*, Kenneth Fearing
10 · *BRIGHTON ROCK*, Graham Greene

Suspense

❖❖

BY MARY HIGGINS CLARK

According to *Webster's Ninth New Collegiate Dictionary,* the definition of suspense is:

1. *the state of being suspended, i.e., held in an undeter-mined or undecided state awaiting further information*
2. *a) mental uncertainty or anxiety*
   b) pleasant excitement as to a decision or outcome
3. *the state or character of being undecided or doubtful*

Doesn't that say it all? Uncertainty, anxiety, pleasant excitement, indecision, doubt. Ergo! We've got the makings of a suspense novel.

I'm often asked why as a writer I chose this field. I guess that from the beginning it chose me. As a child I loved to hear and tell scary stories. The idea of a lighted candle didn't go over big with the resident adults, so evenings when we kids got together, I'd suggest that we turn out all the lights except one tiny one. Then we'd have a contest to determine who could spin the creepiest yarn.

Mine was likely to start like this: "There's a man outside! He's watching us. Don't turn around. Don't let him know that we see him. He's looking through the window. He's coming to murder one of us. Oh, Mary Katherine, I'm sorry, he's pointing at you."

I loved that game.

The first two short stories that I sold were suspense stories only because I happened to have ideas for them. Unfortunately for my bank account I didn't write suspense again for another twenty years. Then when I decided I wanted to try a novel, I looked at my bookshelves and realized that my reading of choice had always been in the suspense field. The shelves were stacked with Agatha Christie, Sir Arthur Conan Doyle, Josephine Tey, Ngaio Marsh, Daphne du Maurier, Rex Stout, John D. MacDonald, etc., etc., etc.

In the fable of Hansel and Gretel, the children dropped smooth pebbles and breadcrumbs in order to find their way back out of the forest. The birds ate the breadcrumbs.

The suspense writer must drop both real clues and red herrings. Much of the enjoyment for the reader is determining which is which. I had become a reasonably astute reader and decided to give it a shot and see if I could make it as a writer in this field.

Then of course comes the question: What's the plot? I'd been raised hearing about the Lindbergh baby kidnapping. We had a summer cottage at Silver Beach in the Bronx and every once in a while when we passed St. Raymond's cemetery my father would point to the table outside its flower shop and say, "And there, my dear, is where the ransom note for that poor little baby was left."

And so I grew up with the memory of that tragic case, the kidnapping of the golden child of the golden couple. I decided that a kidnapped child would be the subject of my first attempt at a suspense novel. Exactly at that time there was a celebrated court case in progress in New York. A beautiful young mother was accused of the deliberate, cold-blooded murder of her two children.

Mention that case and everyone had an opinion, a very strong opinion. I thought back to my first writing course in which the professor had said, "Take an event that is compelling, dramatic, memorable. Ask yourself two questions, 'Suppose?' and 'What if?' and write a fictional version with the nucleus of that event as the starting point."

I'd followed that advice with several dozen short stories. Now that I was attempting a novel that would concern kidnapping, I asked myself: "Suppose, what if, an innocent young mother is accused and found guilty of murdering her two young children? Suppose she is released from prison on a technicality, flees to Cape Cod, remarries and begins a new life? And suppose seven years later to the day of the first tragedy, the children of her second marriage disappear?

I thought it was a good premise and began to envision characters. I like to tell a suspense story in as brief a period as possible.

That book took place in fourteen hours. It took three years to write. I still remember the moment when I finally carried the manuscript under my arm and dropped it off at my agent's office. A couple of months passed. Two publishers turned it down because they felt that children in jeopardy might upset their women readers. Then came that marvelous day when I received the call. Simon & Schuster wanted to buy it. I thought I'd died and gone to heaven.

It is a great honor for me that *Where Are the Children?* has now been included in the suspense category of this publication, especially in view of the other writers whose company I keep.

No one writer can speak for all writers. We choose our subjects and tell our tales in different ways. But if I were asked how I perceive suspense I would say that suspense is created when the ordinary becomes extraordinary, the familiar becomes chilling.

Ten of us meet for dinner once a month to talk about mystery and suspense. We briefly discuss our current work in progress, exchange ideas, methods of research, settings, plots.

We talk about which comes first, plot or character, or if they are synonymous.

One night we talked about the scariest sound.

The suggestions: a scream, a gunshot, shattering glass. . . . Then came the one that I loved: "The house is completely locked up. You're alone in bed. It's late and dark. And the toilet flushes." The familiar became chilling.

For the rest of it, in my own attempts, I love the idea that the reader is one step ahead of the main character and worried about her. "Don't get in the car with him, he's a killer."

I love short chapters and multiple viewpoints. It harkens back to the old days at St. Francis Xavier, where you were given a one-line speaking part and then exited from the stage. Say your piece and get lost.

I want to offer to the reader the sense of being on a roller coaster. Remember as a child when you bought your ticket and immediately your heart started pounding? You knew you were going to be scared.

I want the woman to be in jeopardy.

I want the reader to become engrossed, put aside necessary tasks, stay up too late to finish the book.

Why? Because as a writer I've tried to offer what suspense was meant to be, anxiety and pleasant excitement. I know the other writers chosen for this category have succeeded splendidly! I'm glad that some people think I may have as well.

Hard-Boiled/Private Eye

1 · *The Maltese Falcon,* Dashiell Hammett
2 · *The Big Sleep,* Raymond Chandler
3 · *The Long Goodbye,* Raymond Chandler
4 · *Farewell, My Lovely,* Raymond Chandler
5 · *The Thin Man,* Dashiell Hammett
6 · *Red Harvest,* Dashiell Hammett
7 · *I, the Jury,* Mickey Spillane
8 · *"A" Is for Alibi,* Sue Grafton
9 · *The Lady in the Lake,* Raymond Chandler
10 · *The Doorbell Rang,* Rex Stout

Here's the next ten, FYI:

11 · *The Dreadful Lemon Sky,* John D. MacDonald
12 · *The Chill,* Ross Macdonald
13 · *Eight Million Ways to Die,* Lawrence Block
14 · *Black Cherry Blues,* James Lee Burke
15 · *When the Sacred Ginmill Closes,* Lawrence Block
16 · *The Little Sister,* Raymond Chandler
17 · *The Green Ripper,* John D. MacDonald
18 · *The Glass Key,* Dashiell Hammett
19 · *The Last Good Kiss,* James Crumley
20 · *The Underground Man,* Ross Macdonald

An Eye for an I:

Justice, Morality,
the Nature of the Hard-Boiled Private Detective,
and All That Existential Stuff
by Sue Grafton

I was raised on a steady diet of mystery and detective fiction. During the forties my father, C. W. Grafton, was himself a part-time mystery writer and it was he who introduced me to the wonders of the genre. In my early teens, on the occasions when my parents went out for the evening, I'd be left alone in the house with its tall, narrow windows and gloomy high ceilings. By day surrounding maple trees kept the yard in shadow. By night overhanging branches blocked out the pale of the moon. Usually I sat downstairs in the living room in my mother's small upholstered rocking chair, reading countless mystery novels with a bone-handled butcher knife within easy reach. If I raised my head to listen, I could always hear the nearly imperceptible footsteps of someone coming up the basement stairs.

Mystery novels were the staple of every summer vacation when, released from the rigors of schooldays and homework, I was free to read as much as I liked. I remember long August nights where the darkness came slowly. Upstairs in my bedroom I'd lie in a shortie nightgown with the sheets flung back, reading. The bed lamp threw out a heat of its own and the humidity would press on the bed like a quilt. June bugs battled at the window, an occasional victor forcing its way through the screen. It was in this atmosphere of heightened awareness and beetle-induced suspense that I worked my way from Nancy Drew through Agatha Christie and on to Mickey Spillane. I can still remember the astonishment I felt the night I leaped from the familiarity of Miss Marple into the pagan sensibilities of *I, the Jury*. From Mickey Spillane I turned to James M. Cain, then to Raymond Chandler, Dashiell Hammett, Ross Macdonald, Richard Prather, and John D. MacDonald, a baptism by immersion in the dark poetry of murder. I think I sensed even then that a detective novel offered the perfect blend of ingenuity and intellect, action and artifice.

During the thirties hard-boiled private eyes seemed to be spontaneously generated in pulp fiction like mice in a pile of old rags. After World War II the country was caught up in boom times, a bonanza of growth and cockeyed optimism. "Our boys" came home from overseas and took up their positions on assembly lines. Women surrendered their jobs at defense plants and (brainwashed by the media) returned to Home Sweet Home. In that postwar era of ticky-tacky housing and backyard barbecues, the hard-boiled private eye was a cynical, wisecracking, two-fisted, gun-toting hero. We could identify with this machismo and admire his ruthless principles, his reckless way with a .45. He smoked too much, drank too much, screwed and punched his way through molls and mobsters with devastating effect. In short, he kicked ass. In his own way he was a fictional extension of the jubilance of the times, a man who lived with excess and without regard for consequence. He embodied the exhilaration of the faraway battlefield brought back to home turf.

Through the forties and fifties the hard-boiled private-eye novel was escapist fare, reassuring us by its assertion that there was still danger and excitement, a place where treachery could threaten and heroism could emerge. Despite the mildly depressing lull of the postwar peace, detective fiction proved that adventure was still possible. The core of the hard-boiled private-eye novel was a celebration of the confrontation, as exotic as the blazing guns of the Old West, as familiar as the streets beyond our white picket fences. In fictional terms the hard-boiled private eye provided evidence that the courage of the individual could still make a difference.

Crime in those days had a tabloid quality. Murder was fraught with sensationalism and seemed to take place only in the big cities half a continent away. Justice was tangible and revenge was sweet. With his flat affect, the hard-boiled private eye was the perfect emissary from the dark side of human nature. War had unleashed him. Peace had brought him home. Now he was free to roam the shadowy elements of society. He carried our rage. He championed matters of right and fair play while he violated the very rules the rest of us were forced to embrace. Onto his blank and cynical face we projected our own repressed impulses, feeling both drawn to and repelled by his tough-guy stance.

There was something seductive about the primal power of the hard-boiled narrative, something invigorating about its crude literary style. For all its tone of disdain, the flat monotone of the narrator allowed us to "throw" our own voices with all the skill of ventriloquists. *I* was Mike Hammer. *I* was Sam Spade, Shell Scott, Philip Marlowe, and Lew Archer, strengthened and empowered by the writers' raw-boned prose. Little wonder then that, years later, in a desire to liberate myself from the debilitating process of writing for television, I turned to the hard-boiled private-eye novel for deliverance.

Times have changed. In the years since Mike Hammer's heyday, rage has broken loose in the streets. We live in darker times, where the nightmare has been made manifest. Violence is random, pointless, and pervasive. Passing motorists are gunned down for the vehicles they drive, teens are killed for their jackets and their running shoes. Homicide has erupted on every side of us in a wholesale slaughter of the innocent. Even small-town America has been painted by its bloody brush. The handgun is no longer a symbol of primitive law and order; it is the primogenitor of chaos. The bullet makes its daily rampage, leaving carnage in its wake. We are at the mercy of the lawless. While the cunning of fictional homicide continues to fascinate, its real-life counterpart has been reduced to senseless butchery. Murder is the beast howling in the basement, rustling unleashed in the faraway reaches of our souls.

In this atmosphere of anarchy we are forced to revitalize and reinvent a mythology from which we can draw the comforts once offered us by the law. The fictional adventures of the hard-boiled private eye are still escapist and reassuring, but from a topsy-turvy point of view. The hard-boiled private eye in current fiction represents a clarity and vigor, the immediacy of a justice no longer evident in the courts, an antidote to our confusion and our fearfulness.

In a country where violence is out of control, the hard-boiled private eye exemplifies containment, order, and hope, with the continuing, unspoken assertion that the individual can still make a difference. Here, resourcefulness, persistence, and determination prevail. The P.I. has been transformed from a projection of our vices to the mirror of our virtues. The hard-boiled private eye has come to represent and reinforce not our excess but our moderation. In the current hard-boiled private-eye fiction, there is less alcohol, fewer cigarettes, fewer weapons, greater emphasis on fitness, humor, subtlety, maturity, and emotional restraint. It is no accident that women writers have tumbled onto the playing field, infusing the genre with a pervasive social conscience. Entering the game, too, are countless other private-eye practitioners, writers representing the gay, the African American, the Native American, the Asian American, an uncommon variety of voices now clamoring to be heard.

The hard-boiled private-eye novel is still the classic struggle between good and evil played out against the backdrop of our social interactions. But now we are championed by the knight with a double gender, from talented writers who may be female as well. Women have moved from the role of femme fatale to that of prime mover, no longer relegated to the part of temptress, betrayer, or loyal office help. The foe is just as formidable, but the protagonist has become androgynous, multiracial, embracing complex values of balance and compassion. I do not necessarily maintain that today's hard-boiled hero/ine is cast of finer metal, only that s/he is more diverse, more protean, a multifaceted arbiter of our desires in conflict. Because of this, the hard-boiled private-eye novel is once more rising to the literary forefront, gaining renewed recognition. Now, as before, we are serving notice to the reading public that the genre is not only alive and well, but that we, as its creators, are still adapting, still reacting, and, with wit and perspicacity, we are still marching on.

Police Procedural

1 · *DANCE HALL OF THE DEAD*, Tony Hillerman
2 · *THE LAUGHING POLICEMAN*, Maj Sjöwall and Per Wahlöö
3 · *GORKY PARK*, Martin Cruz Smith
4 · *A THIEF OF TIME*, Tony Hillerman
5 · *THE FIRST DEADLY SIN*, Lawrence Sanders
6 · *LAST SEEN WEARING*, Hillary Waugh
7 · *THE STEAM PIG*, James McClure
8 · *THE CHOIRBOYS*, Joseph Wambaugh
9 · *SHROUD FOR A NIGHTINGALE*, P. D. James
10 · *ICE*, Ed McBain, and *IN THE HEAT OF THE NIGHT*, John Ball (tie)

Police Procedural

❧·❦

*A*lthough I am honored to have *The Choirboys* included on such a distinguished list, I wonder if the tribute is deserved. Many of the critics who overpraised that offbeat novel back in 1975 noted that the book was rather the antithesis of what was called a "police procedural."

At that time I had not read much in the mystery, crime, police, and thriller genres, not even Raymond Chandler! This defect I have since corrected. The books that I did reread prior to starting *The Choirboys* were *Catch-22* and *Slaughterhouse-Five*. I think I realized instinctively that I was not writing a police novel but a war novel. My choirboys were at war with all comers: criminals, police department brass, bureaucrats, the public in general, and especially with themselves.

The manuscript was nothing like my first two novels, *The New Centurions* and *The Blue Knight*. Nor did *The Choirboys* bear any resemblance to my nonfiction book, *The Onion Field*. This novel, my first as a *former* cop, was different. Still at loose ends after having just abandoned a fourteen-year-old career with the Los Angeles Police Department, I was attempting to find a new voice, one with which I could tell a different kind of police story by using gallows humor, satire, hyperbole, and irony. I wanted to tell a very serious story that would make the reader laugh painfully, and not without a bit of embarrassment for having done so.

One thing was certain: The title seemed right. With my first two novels I'd had to endure commentary from people who hadn't read the books and didn't know that *centurions* and *knight* were meant ironically. With *choirboys* nobody had any trouble guessing that the cops portrayed therein would not be cassocked cherubs carrying prayer books. (An exception was reported in the *Irish Times,* wherein a nun from Dublin assigned the novel to her adolescent students, thinking it was a novel with a religious theme.)

But in the beginning there was the manuscript, and after reading it the senior editor at my publishing house was so disgusted that he advised me to abandon the project and try again. I was devastated. Was I merely a cop-writer who could not produce an acceptable book as a nonhyphenated "civilian"? I put the manuscript aside for two months and went on vacation. When I returned, I examined it, telephoned New York, and said, "This is the book. There is no other. You don't have to publish it, but I'm not returning the big advance you paid me. Take it or leave it, this *is* the book that I promised to deliver."

Reluctantly he took it, and it became not only a huge critical success, but one of the biggest bestsellers they'd ever had. I have since learned that there were several junior editors who'd immediately recognized the worth of the manuscript and predicted a blockbuster. A lesson for publishing executives, perhaps: If you hate the *idea* of escargot, it doesn't matter if it's prepared at Cordon Bleu; it will still look like a slimy glop of mollusk that should be stomped on on sight like a black widow spider. I have since used the comedy of the grinning skull in subsequent novels that were also deadly serious at the core, novels such as *The Glitter Dome* and my favorite, *The Secrets of Harry Bright.*

The "proper" police procedural had always demonstrated how the cop acts on the job, but *The Choirboys* attempted to show how the job acts on the cop. The viscera and brain of the choirboy was bared for all to see. Literary critics began talking about something called "police stress." Perhaps *The Choirboys* demonstrated that, despite Hollywood's violent portrayal, police service is not particularly dangerous physically, but *emotionally* it's the most dangerous job on earth. Young people doing urban police work are somewhat prepared to meet the worst of people, but nothing prepares them to meet ordinary people at their worst. It can be particularly horrifying to learn what some "ordinary" people are capable of doing within the confines of their homes.

Very soon, the insidious cop syllogism can take hold: People are garbage; I am a person; it follows therefore that I am . . . And that's where emotional problems start, often resulting in divorce, alcoholism, drug addiction, suicide. Not a pleasant subject to read about *unless* it is camouflaged by dark, defensive, cynical gallows humor, or so I decided. After every traumatic police experience, my choirboys would gather to keen and wail and carouse in boozy sessions called "choir practice." (By the way, I did not invent the term; that's what we called it at the Los Angeles Police Department.)

Finally, I suppose it should be said that I don't care if *The Choirboys* is or is not a proper police procedural. I don't like genre categories anyway. A novel is a novel is a novel. Any of the other authors on this police procedural list could write about the sex lives of sea anemones and make it beguiling, I'm sure. Nowadays, of course, the entire literary world admits that our MWA colleagues are every bit as good as so-called "mainstream" writers, but I wonder if everyone is aware of a significant difference? After attending writers' conferences with each type of animal, I can say for sure: My MWA cohorts are *far* more fun at choir practice!

Espionage/Thriller

1 · *THE SPY WHO CAME IN FROM THE COLD,* John le Carré
2 · *A COFFIN FOR DIMITRIOS,* Eric Ambler
3 · *EYE OF THE NEEDLE,* Ken Follett
4 · *THE DAY OF THE JACKAL,* Frederick Forsyth
5 · *TINKER, TAILOR, SOLDIER, SPY,* John le Carré
6 · *THE THIRTY-NINE STEPS,* John Buchan
7 · *THE IPCRESS FILE,* Len Deighton
8 · *SMILEY'S PEOPLE,* John le Carré
9 · *ROGUE MALE,* Goeffrey Household
10 · *THE THIRD MAN,* Graham Greene

People Who
Live Only in the Mind

BY JOHN GARDNER

"Where do the ideas come from?" That is probably the question most asked of writers of fiction, and it is possibly the question most dreaded. Some authors talk of ideas coming from snippets in the newspapers or an overheard conversation. Laurence Durrell once replied: "God's backside."

Yes, certainly ideas come from such things as newspaper items and overheard conversations, but I for one do not think it is a conscious action. The ideas do not leap unbidden into the mind. Rather, they come in bits and pieces, revealing themselves over a period of time. But what do I know? All authors have their own way of working.

I am aware of some people who must have the entire narrative blocked out in a series of detailed scenes, one leading to the next, with the dénouement well prepared.

Personally I could not work like that. I begin with a germ of a concept and a kind of skeleton map, almost a hieroglyphic. The rest remains hidden, and, of course, I am aware of the fact that I am purposely screening things off from myself. I do not want to know what happens at the end, for I like to make the journey as a reader makes it. Then, once all is done, the long polishing process begins, sometimes over three or four drafts. For me the challenge is, Where do the characters come from? How do you people a novel?

This is the most interesting part of creativity: the author playing God and creating his own Adams, Eves, and snakes, with past, present, and future enshrined within people who exist only on the printed page. Recently, in an after-dinner talk with a psychiatrist, I was struck by his questions regarding the creation of character and my personal—almost Stanislavskian—method, which made the doctor's eyebrows shoot almost to the back of his head. "Very dangerous, identifying deeply with a fictitious character,'' he said. I knew that already, as my wife often complains that I am not myself when working!

Only once has something inexplicable happened to me regarding the creation of a character.

Back in the late 1970s I was commissioned, by Hodder & Stoughton, to do a book, later titled *The Nostradamus Traitor.* I gave them a basic idea, concerning the use of the famous Nostradamus Quatrains, and how they were used, by both the Nazis and the British, in psychological operations during World War II.

The first draft produced the makings of a book set firmly within the framework of the 1939–1945 conflict. I was unhappy with the outcome and felt that I should try to use what I had written as the kernel of a book set in the then-present so that actions in the past would impact on readers in the here and now.

An American friend had told me the story of a visit he had made to the Tower of London and a conversation that had taken place with one of the Yeoman warders—Beefeaters to us mortals. Apparently a German woman had turned up one day and wanted to see the rifle range where her son had been executed as a spy. With some changes I used this as the opening, having the Yeoman warder report the matter, which was routinely sent on to the Security and Secret Intelligent Services.

At that point, without even thinking, I wrote ''The file landed on Herbie Kruger's desk.'' There and then I was able to describe Kruger as though I knew him intimately: his past and present, his foibles and fancies, his outward appearance, interests, quirks—the whole nine yards, as they say.

There was no need to think about it, the character was there, complete, born in a matter of an hour, full of detail. I went on and wrote a whole trilogy with this character as the main protagonist, and resurrected him again in three other books. At this moment he is with me once more with work in progress. This has never happened, before or since, and it is, for me, a unique experience. I have no idea where this much-loved character came from, but he did appear and is utterly real for me.

There is a strange sequel to this story. About a month after *The Nostradamas Traitor* was completed, my wife and I moved to the Republic of Ireland. We arrived in Dublin on Maundy Thursday, where we found that the apartment we were renting was not ready for us. I called a friend for advice regarding hotels and he suggested a remote castle near Wicklow town—an hour or so from Dublin—which was owned by a German couple.

We found the place on a pitch-black night, and it seemed like something out of *Dracula.* I heaved on a large bellpull and from within came the sound of barking dogs, followed by a voice I vaguely recognized, shouting at the dogs. Many bolts seemed to be drawn back and the door finally opened to reveal—yes, you are right—the spit and image of the man I had created as Herbie Kruger: mannerisms, fractured English, and all. I just accept it. The whole thing was so strange that I do not even attempt to analyze it. I only know that it happened and that writing about this character became more and more pleasant after I had met his real-life twin.

Criminal

---

1 · *The Godfather*, Mario Puzo
2 · *The Postman Always Rings Twice*, James M. Cain
3 · *Double Indemnity*, James M. Cain
4 · *Little Caesar*, W. R. Burnett
5 · *In Cold Blood*, Truman Capote
6 · *The Friends of Eddie Coyle*, George V. Higgins
7 · *The Killer Inside Me*, Jim Thompson
8 · *Stick*, Elmore Leonard
9 · *The Talented Mr. Ripley*, Patricia Highsmith
10 · *Prizzi's Honor*, Richard Condon

The Crime Novel

➻-➼

BY RICHARD CONDON

The country's appetite for crime in novels, in movies, and on TV has hardly changed with the times. But crime is no longer light entertainment. Drive-by shootings, children shooting children, indeed the proliferation of American cities competing to be acclaimed as the "crime capital of the world" has overpowered the diversions of the whodunit, the mystery puzzle that was once the ultimate entertainment. A diverting fantasy, the mystery novel ("the butler did it") has been replaced. It has been shouldered aside by murder-for-real.

Crime on the printed page, on the screen, and on the boob tube has become for the nation a how-to-do-it mirror, a distancing from the horror of the real thing, a reflection of "there but for the grace of God go I" upon an enormous audience conditioned by the constant pressure of their overcommunications industry. The detective story has been shouldered aside by the ruffianly crime novel. Just as American sports, religion, and ideals of female beauty have been industrialized, so has crime. "We are bigger than General Motors," said Meyer Lansky, one of the two prime organizers of modern organized crime.

I was drawn to the subject of *Prizzi's Honor* because organized crime was not only an industrialized catchall for the national taste, but it greatly overlapped, and improved upon, all other categories of crime. If Americans are spectators of the national sport of murder, they expect it to be done well, professionally, not be amateurs. As a distant relative of organized sports, which plays such an important part of our lives, we want these crimes we enjoy thirdhand through the overcommunications industry to be carried off with polish and ulitmate professionalism. It is understood in a society where everything is industrialized that people who do their thing for money do it best. That is why there is so little public response to the crime rate of the nation and to the homicide rate up and down one's own street in one's own town. It is the work of amateurs. If a job such as murder is worth doing, it is worth doing well. Hence the total national public fascination with organized crime, each member a criminal professional to his fingertips.

I wrote *Prizzi's Honor* as an annal of crime because of the professionalism of organized criminals. When *they* killed it was for business reasons, something any sound American business community can understand. The annual income of the New York Mafia families alone, excluding the black and Asian practitioners of industrialized crime, exceeded ten billion dollars a year, tax-free. Given that condition, there was nothing personal about the many organizational murders it became necessary to commit, murders that the national overcommunications industry had glamorized from Al Capone and the St. Valentine's Day Massacres forward through Murder, Inc. and John Gotti; an efficiently conceived instrument for settling differences coolheadedly.

Crime is a prime American industry. There is a concerted drive on, surging out of Congress, to eliminate crime, but crime by their definitions, which restrict it almost entirely to amateurs, never to the overly profiting professionals or to politicians and their clients. Crime of the sort that will fill the hundred-odd extra prisons and will justify the hundred thousand extra police officers. Crime that will be committed by the amateurs armed by the National Rifle Association claiming the Second Amendment to the U.S. Constitution as their "right to bear arms," an amendment required over two hundred years ago by a nation in revolution, by people living in isolation threatened by Indians, and because (at that time) there were no supermarkets: Father needed a gun to go out to shoot the groceries. Now those guns are still readily available, legal and handy, but they have been turned upon the rest of us until the United States of America has become the leader in murder in the world.

Crime novels distance us from the corpses that litter the streets of the inner cities and the pain that comes with homicide. By telling the story of crime as it shows itself in so many hundreds of forms, the crime novel in seeking to explain crime makes it much more compatible than it is. Crime novels show the consequence of crime in a more direct way than as it is reported by the overcommunications industry. They must report it and track it and beat it to death, its meaning lost over the months it takes from the execution of a crime to the disposition of the criminal.

The crime novel, like crime, amateur and professional, is here to stay.

Cozy/Traditional

———————— ❦ ————————

1 · *AND THEN THERE WERE NONE*, Agatha Christie
2 · *THE MURDER OF ROGER ACKROYD*, Agatha Christie
3 · *GAUDY NIGHT*, Dorothy L. Sayers
4 · *THE NINE TAILORS*, Dorothy L. Sayers
5 · *MURDER MUST ADVERTISE*, Dorothy L. Sayers
6 · *MURDER ON THE ORIENT EXPRESS*, Agatha Christie
7 · *STRONG POISON*, Dorothy L. Sayers
8 · *CLOUDS OF WITNESS*, Dorothy L. Sayers
9 · *THE THREE COFFINS*, John Dickson Carr
10 · *THE BODY IN THE LIBRARY*, Agatha Christie
Here's the next ten, FYI:
11 · *THE MOVING TOYSHOP*, Edmund Crispin
12 · *THE ABC MURDERS*, Agatha Christie
13 · *I.O.U.*, Nancy Pickard
14 · *THE FRANCHISE AFFAIR*, Josephine Tey
15 · *THE MYSTERIOUS AFFAIR AT STYLES*, Agatha Christie
16 · *TIGER IN THE SMOKE*, Margery Allingham
17 · *DEATH ON THE NILE*, Agatha Christie
18 · *CALAMITY TOWN*, Ellery Queen
19 · *GREEN FOR DANGER*, Christianna Brand
20 · *THE MIRROR CRACK'D*, Agatha Christie

The Cozy/Traditional Mystery

❧❧

BY MARGARET MARON

*I*n the great prewar "Golden Age," Agatha Christie and Dorothy L. Sayers sat on the pinnacle of British mystery fiction and gazed across the Atlantic to the American pinnacle occupied by Dashiell Hammett and Raymond Chandler. They were the classic either/or dyads of the genre; and looking back over fifty years, it is difficult to conjure up the name of any popular crime writer who did not aspire to make it a triumvirate atop one pinnacle or the other.

Since then the genre has divided and redivided into a dozen recognizably different subgenres. But turf wars are still jealously waged, and hairsplitting definitions continue to blur our perceptions.

It is generally agreed that each mystery or crime novel ever written lies somewhere on a straight-line continuum between dreamy romantic suspense and horrific postapocalyptic splatter punk. For convenience we still label as "cozy" or "traditional" that section of the continuum that contains all the mysteries that remind us of Christie and Sayers, who here occupy nine of the top-ten slots in our survey, even though modern practitioners who consider themselves lineal descendants have so extended the parameters that many are now uncomfortable with that label.

If we no longer expect to find a body on the vicarage hearth rug with the villain unmasked at teatime by a blue-blooded sleuth or nosy spinster, what *can* we expect from a traditional mystery these days?

For starters, it will *not* contain graphic, onstage murder, nonstop violence, excessive profanity, or misogynistic sexual values.

Nor will it have a professional sleuth except in the strictest sense. P. D. James's Adam Dalgleish or Tony Hillerman's Jim Chee and Joe Leaphorn may be salaried police officers and Sherlock Holmes and Hercule Poirot may bill themselves as professional consulting detectives, but all function very much like Sayers's Lord Peter Wimsey or Christie's Miss Marple. They rely less on technical hardware and more on their perceptive understanding of the human heart when it succumbs to pride, jealousy, envy, rage, lust, or thwarted desire.

Whereas other categories along the crime-novel continuum may deal with hired killers and random acts of violence, murder here has a familiar face. Characters are seldom mob-connected foot soldiers, hardened ex-cons, pimps, prostitutes, or professional drug dealers who live in the shadow of anarchy. Instead they are fully dimensioned citizens of a mostly law-abiding world. Within a close circle of family, friends, faculty, or firm, these ordinary people find themselves doing extraordinary deeds. (Indeed, such familiarity is recognized by an annual mystery convention that celebrates the new traditions and calls itself Malice Domestic.)

In this classic form, violence is never by happenstance. If there is a drive-by shooting, the reader will soon learn which of the victim's nearest and dearest possess a driver's license. If someone drops dead of poison, the source of that poison is not a toxic industrial accident but Aunt Hermione's pillbox. The murder weapon is more apt to be borrowed from Father's antique collection of rapiers or dueling pistols than stolen from the local pawn shop.

Today's best examples are still ingeniously plotted whodunits. There may be less reliance on the complicated timetables and arcane methods so dear to Christie and Sayers, but most authors do play fair with the reader by showing all the clues available to the novel's sleuth. Yet because modern readers care about more than murder for murder's sake, many novels now play out against a textured backdrop of societal issues and challenge complacent assumptions.

While it is perhaps historically interesting to see that this survey turned up four titles by Agatha Christie and five by Dorothy L. Sayers, it might have been even more interesting if the respondents had also been asked to name their favorite top-ten *living* traditional authors. Today's crowded field is too wonderfully variegated to allow just two authors to so dominate such a list.

Historical

——————— ➤·◄ ———————

1 · *THE DAUGHTER OF TIME,* Josephine Tey

2 · *THE NAME OF THE ROSE,* Umberto Eco

3 · *THE SEVEN PER-CENT SOLUTION,* Nicholas Meyer

4 · *WOBBLE TO DEATH,* Peter Lovesey

5 · *A MORBID TASTE FOR BONES,* Ellis Peters

6 · *TIME AND AGAIN,* Jack Finney

7 · *DEVIL IN A BLUE DRESS,* Walter Mosley

8 · *CROCODILE ON THE SANDBANK,* Elizabeth Peters

9 · *THE DEVIL IN VELVET,* John Dickson Carr

10 · *THE CHINESE NAIL MURDERS,* Robert van Gulik

The Historical Mystery

BY PETER LOVESEY

*P*redictable?

One of the choices was. I would have bet my last English pound on *The Daughter of Time* topping the list of historical mysteries. Back in 1951 Josephine Tey had the engaging idea of confining her detective, Inspector Alan Grant, to a hospital bed after a fall and having him investigate Richard III's alleged murder of the two boy princes in the Tower of London in 1483. This is history as most of us think of it—the fate of kings—but presented as a murder mystery, complete with twists, discoveries, and a surprise ending, though possibly less of a surprise now than when it was written in 1951. The story of Richard III has inspired several other distinguished mystery writers to interpret the evidence in their own way, notably Elizabeth Peters, Guy Townsend, and Jeremy Potter.

In *The Hatchards Crime Companion,* a survey conducted by the British Crime Writers' Association in 1990, *The Daughter of Time* was not only the top historical mystery but the first choice regardless of category. Another of Josephine Tey's novels, *The Franchise Affair,* was ranked eleventh. As a treatment of history as mystery, the latter novel was even more innovative, for it took an eighteenth-century case—the disappearance of Elizabeth Canning—and gave it a twentieth-century setting. There is a great debate among Tey's numerous admirers as to which is her major achievement. One thing is clearly demonstrated in her work: The historical mystery is capable of being presented in a variety of forms.

By a happy coincidence the Elizabeth Canning case leads us to two of the outstanding American pioneers of the historical mystery. In 1945 Lillian de la Torre wrote an account of the case in the form of a novel, *Elizabeth Is Missing, or Truth Triumphant, an Eighteenth Century Mystery,* and she dedicated the book to John

Dickson Carr, whom she described as the trailblazer. De la Torre's *Dr. Sam Johnson, Detector* (1946), for which she is best known, was such a delightful and witty idea that she sustained it through three more collections. I can only assume that the reason she does not feature in the MWA top ten is because they were short stories rather than novels.

Her mentor, John Dickson Carr, must be on anybody's list. He wrote fourteen historical mysteries ranging from the England of Charles II in 1670 to New Orleans in 1912, and many of his mainstream mysteries also reflect his passion for history. He showed what was possible with the form. There is the reconstruction of a real crime in *The Murder of Sir Edmund Godfrey* (1936), the book that blazed the trail for Lillian de la Torre; there is the conceit of employing a celebrity, Wilkie Collins, as the detective in *The Hungry Goblin* (1972); and there are three that ingeniously take modern people back in time—*The Devil in Velvet* (1955), *Fear Is the Same* (1956), and *Fire, Burn!* (1957). Of these *The Devil in Velvet* deservedly gets the MWA vote, a fine re-creation of Stuart England and a testimony to Carr's ability to turn an unlikely premise into a stunning novel of action that somehow preserves its fidelity to history.

The Devil in Velvet leads us logically to Jack Finney's *Time and Again* (1970), in which the hero travels back in time to New York in the 1880s. The outcome, which I had better not reveal, provides the ultimate in solutions. Some purists have objected that the sci-fi elements in the book disqualify it as mystery fiction, but I cannot agree. The test of such a novel is whether it carries conviction; Finney makes the city live and the plot is absorbing.

The Victorian era has exercised a fascination for mystery writers ever since Edgar Allan Poe, Wilkie Collins, and Arthur Conan Doyle immortalized it with their talent. They wrote as contemporaries, describing a world that, if not entirely real, was close enough to reality to be familiar to their readers. It was a world of extremes: the tea parties of polite society and the street cries of the poor. Occasionally crime invaded the drawing rooms and the teacups rattled with terror. The Sherlock Holmes stories have inspired more imitations, pastiches, and parodies than I would care to list. Nicholas Meyer's *The Seven Per-Cent Solution, Being a Reprint from the Reminiscences of John H. Watson, M.D.* (1974) achieved something unusual, a story that paid homage to Conan Doyle with the quality of the prose while taking liberties with Holmes, who meets Sigmund Freud as well as his old antagonist, Moriarty. Personally, I would rather reread a Holmes original for the umpteenth time than dally with a story purporting to be a new adventure, but Meyer's was amusing, resourceful, and very well done.

Readers wishing to be mystified in a Victorian setting *must*—if they haven't already—make the acquaintance of the engaging Amelia Peabody, the Egyptologist adventuress created by Elizabeth Peters. My personal favorite is *The Last Camel Died at Noon* (1991), huge fun and a genuflection to H. Rider Haggard, but I am willing to be persuaded by the MWA ballot that the first of the series, *Crocodile on the Sandbank* (1975), is equally irresistible. Certainly it is a tour de force, playing with the clichés of Victorian adventure fiction in virtuoso style. Each book in this marvelous series has verve and wit, besides being written with the authority of an expert on Egypt. And the plotting is as intricate as a tomb painting.

Ancient Egypt was, of course, the inspiration for more than one of the novels of Agatha Christie, who once said that an archaeologist was the best husband any woman could have—because the older she got, the more interested he was in her. Dame Agatha's *Death Comes as the End* (1944) was an interesting but ultimately disappointing historical mystery. The books in modern settings with archaeology as a theme were more appropriate to her style. The writer setting a mystery in the remote past—before detective methods and police forces were established—has obvious difficulties, but they are not insuperable. A writer fairly new on the scene, Anton Gill, is currently at work on an interesting and well-researched series set in ancient Egypt, of which *City of the Dead* (1993) is the latest.

Another great civilization is represented in the writings of Robert van Gulik. The Judge Dee series, set in T'ang China about A.D.

670, has a plausible hero, a magistrate based on a genuine histori-cal figure, Ti Jen-chieh. Van Gulik was a Dutch diplomat with a knowledge of Chinese who began by translating a case history and later created mysteries of his own. *The Chinese Nail Murders* (1961) is a fine example with wit and scholarship nicely balanced in a satisfying puzzle.

Greece and Rome are not without their fictional detectives ei-ther. Margaret Doody's *Aristotle, Detective* was one of the first of this kind, and *The Silver Pigs* (1990) launched Lindsey Davis's Roman gumshoe, Marcus Didius Falco, on what promises to be a hugely popular series; but we must move on several centuries to the Middle Ages.

Umberto Eco's *The Name of the Rose* (1983), translated from the Italian by William Weaver, had a huge success when it ap-peared. To do it justice, this novel transcends the mystery genre with its discursions and philosophical arguments, but it also works as a whodunit and deservedly earned second place in the MWA's ranking. Eco has not, to date, returned to the mystery, but readers seeking an expertly researched, atmospheric series featuring a monk are well served by the Brother Cadfael books of Ellis Peters, of which *A Morbid Taste for Bones* (1977), the first in the series, is the favorite of the MWA voters. Brother Cadfael, of course, fits into another segment of the mystery genre: He is with Father Brown and Rabbi David Small as an ecclesiastical sleuth.

It is a huge leap from medieval Shrewsbury to Los Angeles in 1948. *Devil in a Blue Dress* (1990), by Walter Mosley, made a terrific impact on publication, winning awards for the best first novel on both sides of the Atlantic. The narrator, Easy Rawlins, is black and unemployed, and the portrayal of murder and cor-ruption in the city of Raymond Chandler's Marlowe is stark and enthralling. The street life throbs with reality. It may be argued that this is more of a period mystery than a historical one (some of us can remember 1948), but by any standard it is a brilliant achievement.

Finally some regrets. I was sorry not to see listed by the MWA, *Lizzie* by Evan Hunter, *Dear Laura* by Jean Stubbs, *Sweet Ade-*

laide by Julian Symons, *A Coffin for Pandora* by Gwendoline Butler, *The Wench is Dead* by Colin Dexter, *Other Paths to Glory* by Anthony Price, and *The Murder of the Maharajah* by H. R. F. Keating. There, you have some extra titles to seek out. They won't disappoint.

Humorous

1 · *FLETCH*, Gregory Mcdonald
2 · *THE HOT ROCK*, Donald E. Westlake
3 · *BANK SHOT*, Donald E. Westlake
4 · *GOD SAVE THE MARK*, Donald E. Westlake
5 · *SKIN TIGHT*, Carl Hiaasen
6 · *REST YOU MERRY*, Charlotte MacLeod
7 · *DANCING AZTECS*, Donald E. Westlake
8 · *BIMBOS OF THE DEATH SUN*, Sharyn McCrumb
9 · *HOME SWEET HOMICIDE*, Craig Rice
10 · *THE MOVING TOYSHOP*, Edmund Crispin

Pebble, Pond, Perspective

➵◆➴

BY GREGORY MCDONALD

*A*ll great works of art, creation, music, the visual arts, writing, including the greatest story ever told, including our own lives, have the element of mystery in them. Don't you agree?

"We are all mysteries awaiting solution," says Fletch.

And all great works of art, creation, have about them a wit, if not ha-ha, chuckle, giggle funny, surely the refined wit of the ironic.

"We are all histories awaiting execution," says Fletch.

There is no better opportunity for social criticism than the mystery novel—it is so pedestrian. It seldom speaks in statistics or to fashion; it speaks of clocks that are wrong and telephones that don't work. It doesn't describe the Constitution as much as the court officer. It speaks less of the capitol [sic] than of the venial.

Purists at the time the first *Fletch* and *Flynn* novels were written complained loudly that humor had no place in the mystery novel. (As usual, the purists were wrong. The sections of Wilkie Collins's *The Moonstone* concerning Miss Clack are as funny as anything written in the nineteenth century or the twentieth.)

". . . in real life," wrote Israel Zangwell (1864–1926), "mysteries occur to real persons with their individual humors, and mysterious circumstances are apt to be complicated by the comic."

In the mid-1970s, when *Fletch* and *Confess, Fletch* were written, the mystery novel may have been sucking in its last oxygen.

There had been a universal cultural revolution. As always with revolutions, this revolution, continuing in the last half of this century, is based initially and profoundly on technology rather than ideology (the bicycle, telephone, car, radio, television, computer, contraceptive pill), significantly changing our perceptions of time and space, our views of God, nature, and each other.

It wasn't just the mystery novel that was struggling for breath.

In any era of profound change there is a time warp in apprehension, comprehension that creates its own ironies, its own wit.

In 1968 Paul Krassner, a founder of the Youth International Party (YIP), said to your reporter: "If you have a cosmic point of view, you have a sense of absurdity."

Had the human race ever had a truly cosmic point of view before? Had we ever before seen Earth from space?

In their cosmic points of view, in their new regard for women, minorities, authority, neither Fletch nor Flynn, although dissimilar from each other, could have existed before the international cultural revolution of the 1960s and 1970s.

Perhaps it was their more advanced, sophisticated apprehension of the deep cultural changes besetting us that was the source of their humor.

After thinking about Fletch's character, his point of view, for a few years, one day I wrote:

> *"What's your name?"*
> *"Fletch."*
> *"What's your full name?"*
> *"Fletcher."*

In these few silly first words of the novel *Fletch* were established a character, a point of view, the tone for volumes to follow.

Subsequently, in chapter three of *Confess, Fletch,* the second *Fletch* novel written, I wrote:

> *"Pardon my pants. I'm fresh from an axe murder."*

And in these few silly words introducing Inspector Francis Xavier Flynn were established a character quite separate from Fletch, a point of view, and the tone for some volumes to follow.

Not having thought about writing a humorous mystery novel, per se, I suppose I have adopted the public's view that the humor in the *Fletch* and *Flynn* novels comes from the characters of Fletch and Flynn themselves.

Now thinking about it, I realize that is not entirely true.

One can no more be funny in a vacuum than the Marquis de Sade could be satisfied by kicking himself in the arse.

Perhaps it was the degree of apprehension regarding profound changes among others, the characters surrounding Fletch and Flynn, that was the source of humor.

Some were seeing the world through the codes and absolutes of an earlier time.

From *Fletch:*

> (*Fletch*) *went straight to the bull room.*
>
> *"Lupo's in back," the sergeant at the typewriter said. "Beating the shit out of a customer."*
>
> *"I'd hate to interrupt him. Someone might read the customer his rights."*
>
> *"Oh, they've been read to him already. Lupo's interpretation of the Supreme Court ruling has been read to him."*
>
> *"How does Lupo's interpretation go?"*
>
> *"You've never heard it? It's really funny. I can't remember all of it. He rattles it off. Something like: 'You have the right to scream, to bleed, to go unconscious and call an attorney when we get done with you; visible injuries, including missing teeth, will be reported, when questioned, as having occurred before we picked you up, et cetera, et cetera.' It scares the shit out of people."*
>
> *"I bet."*

Some were seeing the world with tragic prescience, such as the institutionalized older woman, Louise Habeck (*Fletch Won*), in her Poetry of Violence.

> SOCIAL SECURITY
> *The sidewalks of the city*
> *Offer up without pity*
> *Old ladies to be mugged.*

A pebble falls in a straight line into a still pond and causes a ripple. It means nothing.

The observer, noting the irony of a straight line creating a circle, is important.

Without the pebble and the pond, the straight line and the circle, the observer, however ironic his nature, can be nothing.

It is the pebble, the pond, and the perspective together that create the observation, the irony, the wit.

Perhaps simply putting together the right characters in the right place at the right time is the source of humor.

Pebble, pond, perspective.

In previous centuries some of our citizens went to our western frontier to escape the rules of law. Daily living became so desperate that the only choices were to "laugh, cry, or get your gun."

At this turn of the century, in this place, with the near total collapse of our judicial system, mostly thanks to people who use drugs and the exorbitant profits therefrom, choices (to some people's view) are becoming the same three.

There's little future in crying, or getting guns, for those who do.

There are tears in the mystery, and guns. Neither tears nor guns guarantee our survival.

Our best chance for both sanity and survival is the ability to observe and report the comic, the wit: to laugh.

> *Is humor anger refined?*
> *I've always thought so.*
> *Is the humorous the mystery refined?*
> *What an amusing thought!*

Legal/Courtroom

1 · *PRESUMED INNOCENT,* Scott Turow
2 · *ANATOMY OF A MURDER,* Robert Traver
3 · *WITNESS FOR THE PROSECUTION,* Agatha Christie
4 · *RUMPOLE OF THE BAILEY,* John Mortimer
5 · *THE FIRM,* John Grisham
6 · *TO KILL A MOCKINGBIRD,* Harper Lee
7 · *A TIME TO KILL,* John Grisham
8 · *THE CASE OF THE VELVET CLAWS,* Erle Stanley Gardner
9 · *THE BURDEN OF PROOF,* Scott Turow
10 · *THE CAINE MUTINY,* Herman Wouk

Legal/Courtroom Mystery

➤-➤

BY SCOTT TUROW

*I*n my last four years as an assistant United States attorney, I was a supervisor of other lawyers, the new recruits to our office who sometimes needed training in litigation skills. Accordingly, I occasionally would go to court as an observer. I was supposed to spend a few minutes assuring myself that my younger colleagues knew how to structure a direct examination, to put a leading question on cross, to address a judge with appropriate deference and unfailing civility.

But sitting with the elderly court buffs on the back benches, I frequently lost track of the time. Even though I was not a participant, I discovered that even the most routine trial—for stealing treasury checks or passing small quantities of dope—could be incredibly dramatic. The witnesses and their inquisitors would struggle with the elusiveness of truth, whether it was obscured by shady recollection or the suspect motivations of guilty-pleading collaborators; at the same time the substance of the testimony given was often gripping, this news of how evil somehow happened in the midst of the everyday.

I had gone to law school after a protracted spell in university settings, where the somewhat academic novels I was writing had proved unpublishable. Still searching years later for themes that would give me some hope of getting a novel in print, I decided to write about what I was seeing in court. Here, I thought, was a drama both meaningful and universal. The whole notion of trial by jury meant that the issues explored had to be ones, no matter what their gravity, that citizens, without specialized training, could grasp.

This was the inspiration for *Presumed Innocent,* a perception that for the author the courtroom was a trove of themes both serious and popular. In the first draft of the novel I did not say who had committed the murder but simply narrowed the field of likely suspects to two. That, I reasoned, was how things sometimes happen in the court: you just don't know. That term, "reasonable doubt," describes much of human interaction. There is so much about which we remain perpetually uncertain. But I ultimately realized that if I wanted to exploit the power of the mystery, I would have to defer to its most abiding rules. The mystery offers us a certainty about what occurred that life—and the courtroom—often cannot. Perhaps that is why it has been so long in being taken seriously. At any rate I knew I was committed by form to saying what the jury might have—who'd done it.

Nonetheless, I think that much of the appeal of fiction about the law lies less in certainty than ambiguity. Reasonable doubt is virtually unique among legal doctrines in that it acknowledges the indefiniteness of legal knowledge. Far more often the law claims an authority that we all suspect it lacks. With its neat categories and iron rules, the law often fails to admit conflicting moral claims or the slipperiness of notions like guilt and blame, an ambiguity that storytelling can both acknowledge and dramatize.

Of course, the emergence of so much fiction about lawyers also signals something else: a widespread recognition that lawyers are increasingly important in today's America. As the United States has become more self-consciously pluralistic, as the authority of other institutions—churches, schools, and local communities—has tended to fade, as we have become less discomfited by the law's equation of bruised feelings with money, our resort as a nation to the law has increased. From its rise in the eighteenth century to the present, the novel has always performed an educational function, and there can be no question that law-related novels have gained much attention simply because they respond to public curiosity about an institution that has interfered in all our lives with increasing frequency, to the occasional, if not perpetual, exasperation of us all. No doubt if this compilation were being prepared a decade ago, there would probably not even be a separate category for legal or courtroom mysteries. And I would be just one more person in the back of a courtroom, spellbound.

Part Three

THE EDGAR WINNERS

The Grand Master Award is the highest award given by the Mystery Writers of America and is presented only to individuals who by a lifetime of achievement have proved themselves preeminent in the craft of the mystery and dedicated to the advancement of the genre. The Grand Master Award is not necessarily presented every year.

1994	Lawrence Block	1976	Graham Greene
1993	Donald E. Westlake	1975	Eric Ambler
1992	Elmore Leonard	1974	Ross Macdonald
1991	Tony Hillerman	1973	Judson Philips
1990	Helen McCloy		Alfred Hitchcock
1989	Hillary Waugh	1972	John D. MacDonald
1988	Phyllis A. Whitney	1971	Mignon G. Eberhart
1987	Michael Gilbert	1970	James M. Cain
1986	Ed McBain	1969	John Creasey
1985	Dorothy Salisbury Davis	1967	Baynard Kendrick
		1966	Georges Simenon
1984	John le Carré	1964	George Harmon Coxe
1983	Margaret Millar	1963	John Dickson Carr
1982	Julian Symons	1962	Erle Stanley Gardner
1981	Stanley Ellin	1961	Ellery Queen (Fred Dannay and Manfred B. Lee)
1980	W. R. Burnett		
1979	Aaron Marc Stein	1959	Rex Stout
1978	Daphne du Maurier Dorothy B. Hughes Ngaio Marsh	1958	Vincent Starrett
		1955	Agatha Christie

Best Novel · (NEW CATEGORY AS OF 1954)

All nominees are listed; winners are denoted by **boldface**.

1994

THE SCULPTRESS **by Minette Walters (St. Martin's)**
FREE FALL by Robert Crais (Bantam)
SMILLA'S SENSE OF SNOW by Peter Hoeg (Farrar, Straus & Giroux)
WOLF IN THE SHADOWS by Marcia Muller (Mysterious Press)
THE JOURNEYMAN TAILOR by Gerald Seymour (HarperCollins)

1993

BOOTLEGGER'S DAUGHTER **by Margaret Maron (Mysterious Press)**
BACKHAND by Liza Cody (Doubleday Perfect Crime)
POMONA QUEEN by Kem Nunn (Pocket Books)
32 CADILLACS by Joe Gores (Mysterious Press)
WHITE BUTTERFLY by Walter Mosley (Norton)

1992

A DANCE AT THE SLAUGHTERHOUSE **by Lawrence Block (Wm. Morrow)**
DON'T SAY A WORD by Andrew Klavan (Pocket Books)
I.O.U. by Nancy Pickard (Pocket Books)
PALINDROME by Stuart Woods (HarperCollins)
PRIOR CONVICTIONS by Lia Matera (Simon & Schuster)

1991

NEW ORLEANS MOURNING **by Julie Smith (St. Martin's)**
BONES AND SILENCE by Reginald Hill (Delacorte)
DEADFALL IN BERLIN by R. D. Zimmerman (Donald I. Fine)
FADE THE HEAT by Jay Brandon (Pocket Books)
WHISKEY RIVER by Loren Estleman (Bantam)

1990

BLACK CHERRY BLUES **by James Lee Burke (Little, Brown)**
GOLDILOCKS by Andrew Coburn (Scribner's)
A QUESTION OF GUILT by Frances Fyfield (Pocket Books)
DEATH OF A JOYCE SCHOLAR by Bartholomew Gill (Wm. Morrow)
THE BOOSTER by Eugene Izzi (St. Martin's)

1989

A COLD RED SUNRISE **by Stuart M. Kaminsky (Scribner's)**
JOEY'S CASE by K. C. Contantine (Mysterious Press)
A THIEF OF TIME by Tony Hillerman (Harper & Row)
IN THE LAKE OF THE MOON by David L. Lindsey (Atheneum)
SACRIFICIAL GROUND by Thomas H. Cook (Putnam)

1988

OLD BONES by Aaron Elkins (Mysterious Press)

A TROUBLE OF FOOLS by Linda Barnes (St. Martin's)

NURSERY CRIMES by B. M. Gill (Scribner's)

ROUGH CIDER by Peter Lovesey (Mysterious Press)

THE CORPSE IN OOZAK'S POND by Charlotte MacLeod (Mysterious Press)

1987

A DARK-ADAPTED EYE by Barbara Vine (Bantam)

THE BLIND RUN by Brian Freemantle (Bantam)

COME MORNING by Joe Gores (Mysterious Press)

A TASTE FOR DEATH by P. D. James (Knopf)

THE STRAIGHT MAN by Roger L. Simon (Villard)

1986

THE SUSPECT by L. R. Wright (Viking Penguin)

CITY OF GLASS: THE NEW YORK TRIOLOGY, PART I by Paul Auster (Sun & Moon Press)

A SHOCK TO THE SYSTEM by Simon Brett (Scribner's)

THE TREE OF HANDS by Ruth Rendell (Pantheon)

AN UNKINDNESS OF RAVENS by Ruth Rendell (Pantheon)

1985

BRIARPATCH by Ross Thomas (Simon & Schuster)

THE BLACK SERAPHIM by Michael Gilbert (Harper & Row)

THE TWELFTH JUROR by B. M. Gill (Scribner's)

EMILY DICKINSON IS DEAD by Jane Langton (St. Martin's)

CHESSPLAYER by William Pearson (Viking Penguin)

1984

LA BRAVA by Elmore Leonard (Arbor House)

THE LITTLE DRUMMER GIRL by John le Carré (Knopf)

THE NAME OF THE ROSE by Umberto Eco (Harcourt Brace Jovanovich)

TEXAS STATION by Christopher Leach (Harcourt Brace Jovanovich)

THE PAPERS OF TONY VEITCH by William McIlvanney (Pantheon)

1983

***BILLINGSGATE SHOAL* by Rick Boyer (Houghton Mifflin)**
EIGHT MILLION WAYS TO DIE by Lawrence Block (Arbor House)
SPLIT IMAGES by Elmore Leonard (Arbor House)
THE CAPTAIN by Seymour Shubin (Stein & Day)
KAHAWA by Donald E. Westlake (Viking)

1982

***PEREGRINE* by William Bayer (Congdon & Lattes)**
THE OTHER SIDE OF SILENCE by Ted Allbeury (Scribner's)
DEATH IN A COLD CLIMATE by Robert Barnard (Scribner's)
DUPE by Liza Cody (Scribner's)
THE AMATEUR by Robert Littell (Simon & Schuster)
BOGMAIL by Patrick McGinley (Ticknor & Fields)

1981

***WHIP HAND* by Dick Francis (Harper & Row)**
DEATH OF A LITERARY WIDOW by Robert Barnard (Scribner's)
DEATH DROP by B. M. Gill (Scribner's)
SPY'S WIFE by Reginald Hill (Pantheon)
MAN ON FIRE by A. J. Quinell (Wm. Morrow)

1980

***THE RHEINGOLD ROUTE* by Arthur Maling (Harper & Row)**
DEATH OF A MYSTERY WRITER by Robert Barnard (Scribner's)
FIRE IN THE BARLEY by Frank Parrish (Dodd, Mead)
MAKE DEATH LOVE ME by Ruth Rendell (Doubleday)
A COAT OF VARNISH by C. P. Snow (Scribner's)

1979

***THE EYE OF THE NEEDLE* by Ken Follett (Arbor House)**
THE SNAKE by John Godey (Putnam)
LISTENING WOMAN by Tony Hillerman (Harper & Row)
A SLEEPING LIFE by Ruth Rendell (Doubleday)
THE SHALLOW GRAVE by Jack S. Scott (Harper & Row)

1978

CATCH ME: KILL ME **by William H. Hallahan (Bobbs-Merrill)**
LAIDLAW by William McIlvanney (Pantheon)
NIGHTWING by Martin Cruz Smith (Norton)

1977

PROMISED LAND **by Robert B. Parker (Houghton-Mifflin)**
THE CAVANAUGH QUEST by Thomas Gifford (Putnam)
A MADNESS OF THE HEART by Richard Neely (Crowell)
THE GLORY BOYS by Gerald Seymour (Random House)
THE MAIN by Trevanian (Harcourt-Brace)

1976

HOPSCOTCH **by Brian Garfield (M. Evans)**
THE GARGOYLE CONSPIRACY by Martin Albert (Doubleday)
OPERATION ALCESTIC by Maggie Rennert (Prentice-Hall)
HARRY'S GAME by Gerald Seymour (Random House)
THE MONEY HARVEST by Ross Thomas (Wm. Morrow)

1975

PETER'S PENCE **by Jon Cleary (Wm. Morrow)**
THE MAN WHO LOVED ZOOS by Malcolm Bosse (Putnam)
GOODBYE AND AMEN by Francis Clifford (Harcourt Brace Jovan-
    ovich)
THE SILVER BEARS by Paul E. Erdman (Scribner's)
THE LESTER AFFAIR by Andrew Garve (Harper & Row)

1974

DANCE HALL OF THE DEAD **by Tony Hillerman (Harper & Row)**
THE RAINBIRD PATTERN by Victor Canning (Wm. Morrow)
AMIGO, AMIGO by Francis Clifford (Coward, McCann, Geoghegan)
AN UNSUITABLE JOB FOR A WOMAN by P. D. James (Scribner's)
DEAR LAURA by Jean Stubbs (Stein & Day)

1973

THE LINGALA CODE **by Warren Kiefer (Random House)**
FIVE PIECES OF JADE by John Ball (Little, Brown)
TIED UP IN TINSEL by Ngaio Marsh (Little, Brown)
THE SHOOTING GALLERY by Hugh C. Rae (Coward, McCann, Geoghegan)
CANTO FOR A GYPSY by Martin Cruz Smith (Putnam)

1972

THE DAY OF THE JACKAL **by Frederick Forsyth (Viking)**
THE FLY ON THE WALL by Tony Hillerman (Harper & Row)
SHROUD FOR A NIGHTINGALE by P. D. James (Scribner's)
SIR, YOU BASTARD by G. F. Newman (Simon & Schuster)
WHO KILLED ENOCH POWELL? by Arthur Wise (Harper & Row)

1971

THE LAUGHING POLICEMAN **by Maj Sjöwall and Per Wahlöö (Pantheon)**
THE HOUND AND THE FOX AND THE HARPER by Shaun Herron (Random House)
BEYOND THIS POINT ARE MONSTERS by Margaret Millar (Random House)
MANY DEADLY RETURNS by Patricia Moyes (Holt, Rinehart & Winston)
AUTUMN OF A HUNTER by Pat Stadley (Random House)
HOT ROCK by Donald E. Westlake (Simon & Schuster)

1970

FORFEIT **by Dick Francis (Harper & Row)**
WHERE THE DARK STREETS GO **by Dorothy Salisbury Davis (Scribner's)**
THE OLD ENGLISH PEEP SHOW by Peter Dickinson (Harper & Row)
MIRO by Shaun Herron (Random House)
BLIND MAN WITH A PISTOL by Chester Himes (Wm. Morrow)
WHEN IN GREECE by Emma Lathen (Simon & Schuster)

1969

A CASE OF NEED by Jeffery Hudson (World)

PICTURE MISS SEETON by Heron Carvic (Harper & Row)

GOD SPEED THE NIGHT by Dorothy Salisbury Davis and Jerome Ross (Scribner's)

THE GLASS-SIDED ANT'S NEST by Peter Dickinson (Harper & Row)

THE VALENTINE ESTATE by Stanley Ellin (Random House)

BLOOD SPORT by Dick Francis (Harper & Row)

1968

GOD SAVE THE MARK by Donald E. Westlake (Random House)

LEMON IN THE BASKET by Charlotte Armstrong (Coward-McCann)

THE GIFT SHOP by Charlotte Armstrong (Coward-McCann)

A PARADE OF COCKEYED CREATURES by George Baxt (Random House)

FLYING FINISH by Dick Francis (Harper & Row)

ROSEMARY'S BABY by Ira Levin (Random House)

1967

THE KING OF THE RAINY COUNTRY by Nicolas Freeling (Harper & Row)

ODDS AGAINST by Dick Francis (Harper & Row)

KILLER DOLPHIN by Ngaio Marsh (Little, Brown)

THE BUSY BODY by Donald E. Westlake (Random House)

1966

THE QUILLER MEMORANDUM by Adam Hall (Simon & Schuster)

THE PALE BETRAYER by Dorothy Salisbury Davis (Scribner's)

FUNERAL IN BERLIN by Len Deighton (Putnam)

THE PERFECT MURDER by H. R. F. Keating (Dutton)

THE FAR SIDE OF THE DOLLAR by Ross Macdonald (Knopf)

AIRS ABOVE THE GROUND by Mary Stewart (Wm. Morrow)

1965

THE SPY WHO CAME IN FROM THE COLD **by John le Carré (Coward-McCann)**

THE NIGHT OF THE GENERALS by Hans Helmut Kirst (Harper & Row)
THE FIEND by Margaret Millar (Random House)
THIS ROUGH MAGIC by Mary Stewart (Wm. Morrow)

1964

THE LIGHT OF DAY **by Eric Ambler (Knopf)**

THE MAKE-BELIEVE MAN by Elizabeth Fenwick (Harper & Row)
GRIEVE FOR THE PAST by Stanton Forbes (Doubleday Crime Club)
THE EXPENDABLE MAN by Dorothy B. Hughes (Random House)
THE PLAYER ON THE OTHER SIDE by Ellery Queen (Random House)

1963

DEATH AND THE JOYFUL WOMAN **by Ellis Peters (Doubleday Crime Club)**

THE ZEBRA-STRIPED HEARSE by Ross Macdonald (Knopf)
SEANCE by Mark McShane (Doubleday Crime Club)
THE EVIL WISH by Jean Potts (Scribner's)
KNAVE OF HEARTS by Dell Shannon (Wm. Morrow)
THE BALLAD OF THE RUNNING MAN by Shelley Smith (Harper & Row)

1962

GIDEON'S FIRE **by J. J. Marric (Harper)**

NIGHTMARE by Anne Blaisdell (Harper)
NIGHT OF WENCESLAS by Lionel Davidson (Harper)
THE WYCHERLY WOMAN by Ross Macdonald (Knopf)
THE GREEN STONE by Suzanne Blanc (Harper)

1961

THE PROGRESS OF A CRIME **by Julian Symons (Harper)**

THE TRACES OF BRILLHART by Herbert Brean (Harper)
THE DEVIL'S OWN by Peter Curtis (Doubleday Crime Club)
WATCHER IN THE SHADOWS by Geoffrey Household (Little, Brown)

1960

THE HOURS BEFORE DAWN **by Celia Fremlin (Lippincott)**

THE LIST OF ADRIAN MESSENGER by Philip MacDonald (Doubleday Crime Club)

1959

THE EIGHTH CIRCLE **by Stanley Ellin (Random House)**

THE MADHOUSE IN WASHINGTON SQUARE by David Alexander (Lippincott)

THE WOMAN IN THE WOODS by Lee Blackstock (Doubleday Crime Club)

A GENTLEMAN CALLED by Dorothy Salisbury Davis (Scribner's)

1958

ROOM TO SWING **by Ed Lacy (Harper)**

THE LONGEST SECOND by Bill Ballinger (Harper)

THE NIGHT OF THE GOOD CHILDREN by Marjorie Carleton (Wm. Morrow)

THE BUSHMAN WHO CAME BACK by Arthur Upfield (Doubleday Crime Club)

1957

A DRAM OF POISON **by Charlotte Armstrong (Coward, McCann)**

THE MAN WHO DIDN'T FLY by Margot Bennett (Harper)

1956

BEAST IN VIEW **by Margaret Millar (Random House)**

THE CASE OF THE TALKING BUG by the Gordons (Doubleday Crime Club)

THE TALENTED MR. RIPLEY by Patricia Highsmith (Coward, McCann)

1955

THE LONG GOODBYE **by Raymond Chandler (Houghton Mifflin)**

1954

BEAT NOT THE BONES **by Charlotte Jay (Harper)**

Best First Novel by an American Author
(ORIGINAL CATEGORY BEGUN IN 1946)

1994
A GRAVE TALENT by **Laurie King (St. Martin's)**
THE LIST OF 7 by Mark Frost (Wm. Morrow)
CRIMINAL SEDUCTION by Darian North (Dutton)
THE BALLAD OF ROCKY RUIZ by Manuel Ramos (St. Martin's)
ZADDIK by David Rosenbaum (Mysterious Press)

1993
THE BLACK ECHO by **Michael Connelly (Little, Brown)**
TRAIL OF MURDER by Christine Andreae (St. Martin's)
TRICK OF THE EYE by Jane Stanton Hitchcock (Dutton)
LADYSTINGER by Craig Smith (Crown)

1992
SLOW MOTION RIOT by **Peter Blauner (Wm. Morrow)**
DEADSTICK by Terence Faherty (St. Martin's)
DEADLINE by Marcy Heidish (St. Martin's)
ZERO AT THE BONE by Mary Willis Walker (St. Martin's)
A COOL BREEZE IN THE UNDERGROUND by Don Winslow (St. Martin's)

1991
POST MORTEM by **Patricia Daniels Cornwell (Scribner's)**
COME NIGHTFALL by Gary Amo (Pinnacle)
PASSION PLAY by W. Edward Blain (Putnam)
NOBODY LIVES FOREVER by Edna Buchanan (Random House)
DEVIL IN A BLUE DRESS by Walter Mosley (Norton)

1990
THE LAST BILLABLE HOUR by **Susan Wolfe (St. Martin's)**
HIDE AND SEEK by Barry Berg (St. Martin's)
THE STORY OF ANNIE D. by Susan Taylor Chehak (Houghton-Mifflin)
THE MOTHER SHADOW by Melodie Johnson Howe (Viking)
BLOOD UNDER THE BRIDGE by Bruce Zimmerman (Harper & Row)

1989

CAROLINA SKELETONS **by David Stout (Mysterious Press)**
MURDER ONCE DONE by Mary Lou Bennett (Perseverance Press)
THE MURDER OF FRAU SCHUTZ by J. Madison Davis (Walker)
A GREAT DELIVERANCE by Elizabeth George (Bantam)
JULIAN SOLO by Shelly Reuben (Dodd, Mead)

1988

DEATH AMONG STRANGERS **by Deidre S. Laiken (Macmillan)**
DETECTIVE by Parnell Hall (Donald I. Fine)
HEAT LIGHTNING by John Lantigua (Putnam)
LOVER MAN by Dallas Murphy (Scribner's)
THE SPOILER by Domenic Stansberry (Atlantic Monthly Press)

1987

NO ONE RIDES FOR FREE **by Larry Beinhart (Wm. Morrow)**
LOST by Gary Devon (Knopf)
RICEBURNER by Richard Hyer (Scribner's)
FLOATER by Joseph Koenig (Mysterious Press)
DEAD AIR by Mike Lupica (Villard)

1986

WHEN THE BOUGH BREAKS **by Jonathan Kellerman (Atheneum)**
THE GLORY HOLE MURDERS by Tony Fennelly (Carroll & Graf)
SLEEPING DOG by Dick Lochte (Arbor House)
THE ADVENTURE OF THE ECTOPLASMIC MAN by Daniel Stashower (Wm. Morrow)

1985

STRIKE THREE, YOU'RE DEAD **by R. D. Rosen (Walker)**
A CREATIVE KIND OF KILLER by Jack Early (Franklin Watts)
FOUL SHOT by Doug Hornig (Scribner's)
SWEET, SAVAGE DEATH by Orania Papazoglou (Doubleday Crime Club)
SOMEONE ELSE'S GRAVE by Alison Smith (St. Martin's)

1984
***THE BAY PSALM BOOK MURDER* by Will Harriss (Walker)**
THE GOLD SOLUTION by Herbert Resnicow (St. Martin's)
RED DIAMOND, PRIVATE EYE by Mark Schorr (St. Martin's)
CAROLINE MINUSCULE by Andrew Taylor (Dodd, Mead)
DEAD MAN'S THOUGHTS by Carolyn Wheat (St. Martin's)

1983
***THE BUTCHER'S BOY* by Thomas Perry (Scribner's)**
BY FREQUENT ANGUISH by S. F. X. Dean (Walker)
UNHOLY COMMUNION by Richard Hughes (Doubleday)
IN THE HEAT OF THE SUMMER by John Katzenbach (Atheneum)
TWO IF BY SEA by Ernest Savage (Scribner's)

1982
***CHIEFS* by Stuart Woods (Norton)**
GIANT KILLER by Vernon Tom Hyman (Marek)
NOT A THROUGH STREET by Ernest Larsen (Random House)
THE BLACK GLOVE by Geoffrey Miller (Viking)
MURDER AT THE RED OCTOBER by Anthony Olcott (Academy Chicago)

1981
***THE WATCHER* by K. Nolte Smith (Coward, McCann, Geoghegan)**
WINDS OF THE OLD DAYS by Betsy Aswald (Dial)
THE REMBRANDT PANEL by Oliver Banks (Little, Brown)
DOUBLE NEGATIVE by David Carkeet (Dial)
THE OTHER ANN FLETCHER by Susanne Jaffe (NAL)

1980
***THE LASKO TANGENT* by Richard North Patterson (Norton)**
NIGHT TRAINS by Peter Heath Fine (Lippincott)
FOLLOW THE LEADER by John Logue (Crown)

1979

KILLED IN THE RATINGS by **William L. DeAndrea (Harcourt Brace Jovanovich)**

THE SCOURGE by Thomas L. Dunne (Coward, McCann & Geoghegan)

FALLING ANGEL by William Hjortsberg (Harcourt Brace Jovanovich)

BLOOD SECRETS by Craig Jones (Harper & Row)

THE MEMORY OF EVA RYKER by Donald A. Stanwood (Coward, McCann & Geoghegan)

1978

A FRENCH FINISH by **Robert Ross (Putnam)**

DEWEY DECIMATED by Charles A. Goodrun (Crown)

THE FAN by Bob Randall (Random House)

1977

THE THOMAS BERRYMAN NUMBER by **James Patterson (Little, Brown)**

YOUR DAY IN THE BARREL by Alan Furst (Atheneum)

STRAIGHT by Steve Knickmeyer (Random House)

THE BIG PAY-OFF by Janice Law (Houghton-Mifflin)

FINAL PROOF by Marie R. Reno (Harper & Row)

1976

THE ALVAREZ JOURNAL by **Rex Burns (Harper & Row)**

WALTZ ACROSS TEXAS by Max Crawford (Farrar, Straus & Giroux)

HARMATTAN by Thomas Klop (Bobbs-Merrill)

PAPERBACK THRILLER by Lynn Meyer (Random House)

THE DEVALINO CAPER by A. J. Russell (Random House)

1975

FLETCH by **Gregory Mcdonald (Bobbs-Merrill)**

SATURDAY GAMES by Brown Meggs (Random House)

TARGET PRACTICE by Nicholas Meyer (Harcourt Brace Jovanovich)

THE KREUTZMAN FORMULA by Virgil Scott and Dominic Koski (Simon & Schuster)

THE JONES MAN by Vern E. Smith (Henry Regnery)

1974

THE BILLION DOLLAR SURE THING by Paul E. **Erdman (Scribner's)**
KICKED TO DEATH BY A CAMEL by Clarence Jackson (Harper & Row)
SOMEONE'S DEATH by Charles Larson (Lippincott)
MANY HAPPY RETURNS by Justin Scott (David McKay)
MAN ON A STRING by Michael Wolfe (Harper & Row)

1973

SQUAW POINT by R. H. **Shimer (Harper & Row)**
A PERSON SHOULDN'T DIE LIKE THAT by Arthur Goldstein (Random House)
THE DEAD OF WINTER by William H. Hallahan (Bobbs-Merrill)
BOX 100 by Frank Leonard (Harper & Row)
THE HEART OF THE DOG by Thomas A. Roberts (Random House)

1972

FINDING MAUBEE by A. H. Z. **Carr (Putnam)**
TO SPITE HER FACE by Hildegarde Dolson (Lippincott)
ASK THE RIGHT QUESTION by Michael Z. Lewin (Putnam)
THE STALKER by Bill Pronzini (Random House)
GYPSY IN AMBER by Martin Cruz Smith (Putnam)

1971

THE ANDERSON TAPES by Lawrence **Sanders (Putnam)**
INCIDENT AT 125TH STREET by J. E. Brown (Doubleday)
TAKING GARY FELDMAN by Stanley Cohen (Putnam)
THE BLESSING WAY by Tony Hillerman (Harper & Row)
THE NAKED FACE by Sidney Sheldon (Wm. Morrow)

1970

A TIME FOR PREDATORS by Joe **Gores (Random House)**
YOU'LL LIKE MY MOTHER by Naomi Hintze (Putnam)
QUICKSAND by Myrick Land (Harper & Row)

1969

TIE: *SILVER STREET* by E. Richard Johnson (Harper & Row) and *THE BAIT* by Dorothy Uhnak (Simon & Schuster)

THE DINOSAUR by Lawrence Kamarck (Random House)

1968

ACT OF FEAR by Michael Collins (Dodd, Mead)

HELL GATE by James Dawson (McKay)

MORTISSIMO by P. E. H. Dunston (Random House)

THE TIGERS ARE HUNGRY by Charles Early (Wm. Morrow)

THE KILLING SEASON by John Redgate (Trident)

1967

THE COLD WAR SWAP by Ross Thomas (Morrow)

FANCY'S KNELL by Babs Deal (Doubleday)

A KIND OF TREASON by Robert S. Elegant (Holt, Rinehart & Winston)

THE PEDESTAL by George Lanning (Harper & Row)

1966

IN THE HEAT OF THE NIGHT by John Ball (Harper & Row)

THE EXPENDABLE SPY by Jack D. Hunter (Dutton)

THE FRENCH DOLL by Vincent McConner (Hill & Wang)

BEFORE THE BALL WAS OVER by Alexandra Roudybush (Doubleday Crime Club)

1965

FRIDAY THE RABBI SLEPT LATE by Harry Kemelman (Crown)

IN THE LAST ANALYSIS by Amanda Cross (Macmillan)

THE GRAVEMAKER'S HOUSE by Rubin Weber (Harper & Row)

1964

FLORENTINE FINISH by Cornelius Hirschberg (Harper & Row)

THE FIFTH WOMAN by H. Fagyas (Doubleday Crime Club)

THE PROWLER by Frances Rickett (Simon & Schuster)

THE NEON HAYSTACK by James M. Ullman (Simon & Schuster)

1963

THE FUGITIVE by Robert L. Fish (Simon & Schuster)

COUNTERWEIGHT by Daniel Broun (Holt, Rinehart & Winston)

THE CHASE by Richard Unekis (Walker)

1962

THE GREEN STONE by Suzanne Blanc (Harper)

FELONY TANK by Malcolm Braley (Gold Medal)

CLOSE HIS EYES by Olivia Dwight (Harper)

THE CIPHER by Alex Gordon (Simon & Schuster)

NIGHT OF THE KILL by Breni James (Simon & Schuster)

SHOCK TREATMENT by Winfred Van Atta (Doubleday Crime Club)

1961

THE MAN IN THE CAGE by John Holbrooke Vance (Random House)

THE MARRIAGE CAGE by William Johnston (Lyle Stuart)

THE KILLING AT BIG TREE by David McCarthy (Doubleday)

CASE PENDING by Dell Shannon (Harper)

THE MERCENARIES by Donald E. Westlake (Random House)

1960

THE GREY FLANNEL SHROUD by Henry Slesar (Random House)

A DREAM OF FALLING by Mary O. Rank (Houghton-Mifflin)

1959

THE BRIGHT ROAD TO FEAR by Richard Martin Stern (Ballantine)

THE MAN WHO DISAPPEARED by Edgar J. Bohle (Random House)

DEATH OF A SPINSTER by Frances Duncombe (Scribner's)

NOW WILL YOU TRY FOR MURDER? by Harry Olesker (Simon & Schuster)

1958

KNOCK AND WAIT A WHILE by William Rawle Weeks (Houghton-Mifflin)

BAY OF THE DAMNED by Warren Carrier (John Day)

ROOT OF EVIL by James Cross (Messner)

1957
Rebecca's Pride **by Donald McNutt Douglass (Harper)**

1956
The Perfectionist **by Lane Kauffman (Lippincott)**
In His Blood by Harold R. Daniels (Dell)
Much Ado About Murder by Fred Levon (Dodd, Mead)

1955
Go, Lovely Rose **by Jean Potts (Scribner's)**

1954
A Kiss Before Dying **by Ira Levin (Simon & Schuster)**

1953
Don't Cry for Me **by William Campbell Gault and E. P. Dutton publisher**
The Inward Eye by Peggy Bacon (Scribner's)

1952
Strangle Hold **by Mary McMullen (Harper)**
Carry My Coffin Slowly by Lee Herrington (Simon & Schuster)
The Christmas Card Murders by David William Meredith (Knopf)
Cure It with Honey by Thurston Scott (Harper)
The Eleventh Hour by Robert B. Sinclair (Mill)

1951
Nightmare in Manhattan **by Thomas Walsh (Little, Brown)**
Strangers on a Train by Patricia Highsmith (Harper)
Happy Holiday! by Thaddeus O'Finn (Rinehart)
The House Without a Door by Thomas Sterling (Simon & Schuster)

1950

WHAT A BODY **by Alan Green (Simon & Schuster)**

THE END IS KNOWN by Goeffrey Holiday Hall (Simon & Schuster)

WALK THE DARK STREETS by William Krasner (Harper)

THE SHADOW AND THE BLOT by N. D. Lobell and G. G. Lobell (Harper)

THE INNOCENT by Evelyn Piper (Simon & Schuster)

THE DARK LIGHT by Bart Spicer (Dodd, Mead)

1949

THE ROOM UPSTAIRS **by Mildred Davis (Simon & Schuster)**

WILDERS WALK AWAY by Herbert Brean (Wm. Morrow)

SHOOT THE WORKS by Richard Ellington (Wm. Morrow)

1948

THE FABULOUS CLIPJOINT **by Fredric Brown (Dutton)**

1947

THE HORIZONTAL MAN **by Helen Eustis (Harper)**

1946

WATCHFUL AT NIGHT **by Julius Fast (Rinehart & Co.)**

Best Original Paperback · (NEW CATEGORY AS OF 1970)

1994

DEAD FOLK'S BLUES **by Steven Womack (Ballantine)**

THE SERVANT'S TALE by Margaret Frazer (Jove/Berkley)

TONY'S JUSTICE by Eugene Izzi (Bantam)

BEYOND SARU by T. A. Roberts (Cliffhanger)

EVERYWHERE THAT MARY WENT by Lisa Scottoline (Harper Paperbacks)

1993

A Cold Day for Murder **by Dana Stabenow (Berkley)**
Principal Defense by Gini Hartzmark (Ivy)
The Good Friday by Lee Harris (Fawcett)
Shallow Graves by William Jefferies (Avon)
Night Cruise by Billie Sue Mosiman (Jove)

1992

Dark Maze **by Thomas Adcock (Pocket Books)**
Murder in the Dog Days by P. M. Carlson (Bantam)
Cracking Up by Ed Naha (Pocket Books)
Midtown North by Christopher Newman (Fawcett)
Fine Distinctions by Deborah Valentine (Avon)

1991

The Man Who Would Be F. Scott Fitzgerald **by David Handler (Bantam)**
Comeback by L. L. Enger (Pocket Books)
Not a Creature Was Stirring by Jane Haddam (Bantam)
Dead in the Scrub by B. J. Oliphant (Fawcett)
SPQR by John Maddox Roberts (Avon)

1990

The Rain **by Keith Peterson (Bantam)**
Manhattan Is My Beat by Jeffery Wilds Deaver (Bantam)
King of the Hustlers by Eugene Izzi (Bantam)
Hot Wire by Randy Russell (Bantam)
A Collector of Photographs by Deborah Valentine (Bantam)

1989

The Telling of Lies **by Timothy Findley (Dell)**
Judgment by Fire by Fredrick D. Huebner (Fawcett)
A Radical Departure by Lia Matera (Bantam)
The Trapdoor by Keith Peterson (Bantam)
Preacher by Ted Thackrey, Jr. (Jove)

1988
***BIMBOS OF THE DEATH SUN* by Sharyn McCrumb (TSR)**
THE MONKEY'S RAINCOAT by Robert Crais (Bantam)
DEADLY INTRUSION by Walter Dillon (Bantam)
THE LONG WAY TO DIE by James N. Frey (Bantam)
BULLSHOT by Gabrielle Kraft (Pocket Books)

1987
***THE JUNKYARD DOG* by Robert Campbell (Signet)**
THE CAT WHO SAW RED by Lilian Jackson Braun (Jove)
HAZZARD by R. D. Brown (Bantam)
RONIN by Nick Christian (Tor)
SHATTERED MOON by Kate Green (Dell)

1986
***PIGS GET FAT* by Warren Murphy (NAL)**
POVERTY BAY by Earl W. Emerson (Avon)
BROKEN IDOLS by Sean Flannery (Charter)
BLUE HERON by Philip Ross (Tor)
BLACK GRAVITY by Conall Ryan (Ballantine)

1985
***GRANDMASTER* by Warren Murphy and Molly Cochran (Pinnacle)**
THE KEYS TO BILLY TILLIO by Eric Blau (Pinnacle)
THE SEVENTH SACRAMENT by Roland Cutler (Dell)
WORDS CAN KILL by Kenn Davis (Fawcett Crest)
BLACK KNIGHT IN RED SQUARE by Stuart M. Kaminsky (Charter)

1984
***MRS. WHITE* by Margaret Tracy (Dell)**
FALSE PROPHETS by Sean Flannery (Charter)
KILL FACTOR by Richard Harper (Fawcett)
TRACE by Warren Murphy (Signet)
HUNTER by Eric Sauter (Avon)

1983

***TRIANGLE* by Teri White (Ace/Charter)**
VITAL SIGNS by Ralph Burrows, M.D. (Fawcett)
CLANDESTINE by James Ellroy (Avon)
THE MISSING AND THE DEAD by Jack Lynch (Fawcett)

1982

***THE OLD DICK* by L. A. Morse (Avon)**
DEADLINE by John Dunning (Fawcett)
THE UNFORGIVEN by Patricia J. MacDonald (Dell)
PIN by Andrew Neiderman (Pocket Books)
DEAD HEAT by Ray Obstfeld (Charter)

1981

***PUBLIC MURDERS* by Bill Granger (Jove)**
BLOOD INNOCENTS by Thomas H. Cook (Playboy)
LOOKING FOR GINGER NORTH by John Dunning (Fawcett)
TOUGH LUCK, L.A. by Murray Sinclair (Pinnacle)

1980

***THE HOG MURDERS* by William L. DeAndrea (Avon)**
THE KREMLIN CONSPIRACY by Sean Flannery (Charter)
VORTEX by David Heller (Avon)
THE QUEEN IS DEAD by Glen Keger (Jove)
THE INFERNAL DEVICE by Michael Kurland (NAL)

1979

***DECEIT AND DEADLY LIES* by Frank Bandy (Charter)**
STUD GAME by David Anthony (Pocket Books)
THE SWITCH by Elmore Leonard (Bantam)
HEARTSTONE by Philip Margolin (Pocket Books)
CHARNEL HOUSE by Graham Masterton (Pinnacle)

1978

THE QUARK MANEUVER **by Mike Jahn (Ballantine)**
TIME TO MURDER AND CREATE by Lawrence Block (Dell)
THE TERRORIZERS by Donald Hamilton (Gold Medal)
THEY'VE KILLED ANNA by Mark Olden (Signet)

1977

CONFESS, FLETCH **by Gregory Mcdonald (Avon)**
THE CAPTIVE CITY by Daniel Da Cruz (Ballantine)
THE RETALIATORS by Donald Hamilton (Fawcett)
FREEZE FRAME by R. R. Irvine (Popular Library)
THE DARK SIDE by Ken Davis and John Stanley (Avon)

1976

AUTOPSY **by John R. Feegel (Avon)**
THE SET-UP by Robin Moore and Milt Machlin (Pyramid)
CHARLIE'S BACK IN TOWN by Jacqueline Park (Popular Library)
THE MIDAS COFFIN by Simon Quinn (Dell)
THE ASSASSINATION by David Vowell (Bantam)

1975

THE CORPSE THAT WALKED **by Roy Winsor (Fawcett)**
WHO KILLED MR. GARLAND'S MISTRESS? by Richard Forrest (Pinnacle)
JUMP CUT by R. R. Irvine (Popular Library)
THE GRAVY TRAIN HIT by Curtis Stevens (Dell)
FLATS FIXED—AMONG OTHER THINGS by Don Tracy (Pocket Books)

1974

DEATH OF AN INFORMER **by Will Perry (Pyramid)**
THE MEDITERRANEAN CAPER by Clive Cussler (Pyramid)
DEADLOCKED! by Leo P. Kelley (Gold Medal)
STARLING STREET by Dinah Palmtag (Dell)
THE BIG FIX by Roger L. Simon (Straight Arrow)

1973

THE INVADER by Richard Wormser (Gold Medal)
NOT DEAD YET by Daniel Banko (Gold Medal)
THE SMITH CONSPIRACY by Richard Neely (Signet)
POWER KILL by Charles Runyon (Gold Medal)

1972

FOR MURDER I CHARGE MORE by Frank McAuliffe (Ballantine)
THE WHITE WOLVERINE CONTRACT by Philip Atlee (Gold Medal)
SPACE FOR HIRE by William F. Nolan (Lancer Books)
NOR SPELL, NOR CHARM by Alicen White (Lancer Books)
AND THE DEEP BLUE SEA by Charles Williams (Signet)

1971

FLASHPOINT by Dan J. Marlowe (Gold Medal)
THE DROWNING by Jack Ehrlich (Pocket Books)
O.D. AT SWEET CLAUDE'S by Matt Gattzden (Belmont)
AFTER THINGS FELL APART by Ron Goulart (Ace)
GRAVE DESCEND by John Lange (Signet)
MAFIOSO by Peter McCurtin (Belmont)

1970

THE DRAGON'S EYE by Scott C. S. Stone (Gold Medal)
ASSAULT ON MING by Alan Caillou (Avon)
THE GOVERNESS by Elsie Cromwell (Paperback Library)
A PLAGUE OF SPIES by Michael Kurland (Pyramid)
THE SOUR LEMON SCORE by Richard Stark (Gold Medal)

Best Fact Crime · (CATEGORY BEGUN IN 1948)

1994

UNTIL THE TWELFTH OF NEVER by Bella Stumbo (Pocket Books)
LINDBERGH: THE CRIME by Noel Behn (Atlantic Monthly/Grove)
FINAL JUSTICE by Steven Naifeh and Gregory White Smith (Dutton)
THE MISBEGOTTEN SON by Jack Olsen (Delacorte)
GONE IN THE NIGHT by David Protess and Rob Warden (Delacorte)

1993

SWIFT JUSTICE **by Harry Farrell (St. Martin's)**

THE TRUNK MURDERESS: WINNIE RUTH JUDD by Jana Bommersbach (Simon & Schuster)

BLOOD ECHOES by Thomas H. Cook (Dutton)

EVERYTHING SHE EVER WANTED by Ann Rule (Simon & Schuster)

MY HUSBAND'S TRYING TO KILL ME by Jim Schutze (HarperCollins)

1992

HOMICIDE: A YEAR ON THE KILLING STREETS **by David Simon (Houghton-Mifflin)**

WITNESSES FROM THE GRAVE: THE STORIES BONES TELL by Christopher Joyce and Eric Stover (Little, Brown)

BOSS OF BOSSES: THE FALL OF THE GODFATHER: THE FBI AND PAUL CASTELLANO by Joseph F. O'Brien and Andris Kurins (Simon & Schuster)

DEN OF THIEVES by James B. Stewart (Simon & Schuster)

DEATH OF ELVIS: WHAT REALLY HAPPENED by Charles C. Thompson II and James P. Cole (Delacorte)

1991

IN A CHILD'S NAME **by Peter Maas (Simon & Schuster)**

GOOMBATA by John Cummings and Ernest Volkman (Little, Brown)

BEYOND REASON by Ken Englade (St. Martin's)

A DEATH IN WHITE BEAR LAKE by Barry Siegel (Bantam)

1990

DOC: THE RAPE OF THE TOWN OF LOVELL **by Jack Olsen (Atheneum)**

THE DEATH SHIFT: THE TRUE STORY OF NURSE GENENE JONES AND THE TEXAS BABY MURDERS by Peter Elkind (Viking)

MURDER IN LITTLE EGYPT by Darcy O'Brien (Wm. Morrow)

THE BLOODING: THE TRUE STORY OF THE NARBOROUGH VILLAGE MURDERS by Joseph Wambaugh (Perigord/Morrow)

WASTED: THE PREPPIE MURDER by Linda Wolfe (Simon & Schuster)

1989

IN BROAD DAYLIGHT **by Harry N. MacLean (Harper & Row)**

FAMILY OF SPIES: INSIDE THE JOHN WALKER SPY RING by Peter Earley (Bantam)

THE COCAINE WARS by Paul Eddy with Hugo Sabogal and Sara Walden (Norton)

MONKEY ON A STICK by John Hubner and Lindsey Gruson (Harcourt Brace Jovanovich)

A GATHERING OF SAINTS by Robert Lindsey (Simon & Schuster)

1988

CBS MURDERS **by Richard Hammer (Wm. Morrow)**

THE MAN WHO ROBBED THE PIERRE by Ira Berkow (Atheneum)

DREAMS OF ADA by Robert Mayer (Viking)

TALKED TO DEATH by Stephen Singular (Beechtree Books/Morrow)

ENGAGED TO MURDER by Loretta Schwartz-Nobel (Viking)

1987

CARELESS WHISPERS: THE TRUE STORY OF A TRIPLE MURDER AND THE DETERMINED LAWMAN WHO WOULDN'T GIVE UP **by Carlton Stowers (Taylor)**

INCIDENT AT BIG SKY: SHERIFF JOHNNY FRANCE AND THE MOUNTAIN MEN by Johnny France and Malcolm McConnell (Norton)

UNVEILING CLAUDIA: A TRUE STORY OF SERIAL MURDER by Daniel Keyes (Bantam)

THE POISON TREE: A TRUE STORY OF FAMILY VIOLENCE AND REVENGE by Alan Prendergast (Putnam)

WISEGUY: LIFE IN A MAFIA FAMILY by Nicholas Pileggi (Simon & Schuster)

1986

SAVAGE GRACE **by Natalie Robins and Steven M. L. Aronson (Wm. Morrow)**

NUTCRACKER: MONEY, MADNESS, MURDER: A FAMILY ALBUM by Shana Alexander (Doubleday)

SOMEBODY'S HUSBAND, SOMEBODY'S SON: THE STORY OF THE YORKSHIRE RIPPER by Gordon Burn (Viking Penguin)

AT MOTHER'S REQUEST: A TRUE STORY OF MONEY, MURDER AND BETRAYAL by Jonathan Coleman (Atheneum)

THE MURDER OF A SHOPPING BAG LADY by Brian Kates (Harcourt Brace Jovanovich)

THE AIRMAN AND THE CARPENTER: THE LINDBERGH KIDNAPPING AND THE FRAMING OF RICHARD HAUPTMANN by Ludovic Kennedy (Viking Penguin)

1985

DOUBLE PLAY: THE SAN FRANCISCO CITY HALL KILLINGS **by Mike Weiss (Addison-Wesley)**

MURDER AT THE MET by David Black (Dial Press)

EVIDENCE OF LOVE: A TRUE STORY OF PASSION AND DEATH IN THE SUBURBS by John Bloom and Jim Atkinson (Texas Monthly Press)

EARTH TO EARTH by John Cornwell (Ecco Press)

THE MOLINEUX AFFAIR by Jane Pejsa (Kenwood Publishing)

1984

VERY MUCH A LADY **by Shana Alexander (Little, Brown)**

JUDGMENT DAY by Bob Lancaster and B. C. Hall (Putnam)

DEADLY FORCE by Lawrence O'Donnell, Jr. (Wm. Morrow)

SON by Jack Olsen (Atheneum)

THE VON BULOW AFFAIR by William Wright (Delacorte)

1983

THE VATICAN CONNECTION by **Richard Hammer (Holt, Rinehart & Winston)**

SOMEBODY IS LYING: THE STORY OF DOCTOR X. by Myron Farber (Doubleday)

INDECENT EXPOSURE by David McClintock (Wm. Morrow)

DEADLY INTENTIONS by William Randolph Stevens (Condon & Weed)

BIG BUCKS by Ernest Tidyman (Norton)

1982

THE STING MAN by **Robert W. Greene (Dutton)**

BY REASON OF DOUBT by Ellen Godfrey (Clarke, Irwin & Co.)

THE MINDS OF BILLY MILLIGAN by Daniel Keyes (Random House)

THE DAY THEY STOLE THE MONA LISA by Seymour V. Reit (Summit)

PAPA'S GAME by Gregory Wallace (Rawson Wade)

1981

A TRUE DELIVERANCE by **Fred Harwell (Knopf)**

ASSASSINATION OF EMBASSY ROW by John Dinges and Saul Landeau (Pantheon)

THE TRIAL OF POLICEMAN THOMAS SHEA by Thomas Hawser (Viking)

1980

THE FALCON AND THE SNOWMAN by **Robert Lindsey (Simon & Schuster)**

ANYONE'S DAUGHTER by Shana Alexander (Viking)

BLOOD WILL TELL by Gary Cartwright (Harcourt Brace Jovanovich)

SENTENCED TO DIE by Stephen H. Gettinger (Macmillan)

ZEBRA by Clark Howard (Marek)

1979

TIL DEATH DO US PART by **Vincent Bugliosi and Ken Hurwitz (Norton)**

WHY HAVE THEY TAKEN OUR CHILDREN? by Jack W. Baugh and Jefferson Morgan (Delacorte)

CRIMINAL VIOLENCE by Charles Silberman (Random House)

PERJURY by Alan Weinstein (Knopf)

1978

BY PERSONS UNKNOWN **by George Jonas and Barbara Amiel
(Grove Press)**

JUSTICE CRUCIFIED by Roberta S. Feuerlicht (McGraw-Hill)

CLOSING TIME by Lacey Fosburgh (Delacorte)

SIX AGAINST THE ROCK by Clark Howard (Dial Press)

THE VOICE OF GUNS by Vin McLellan and Paul Avery (Putnam)

1977

BLOOD AND MONEY **by Thomas Thompson (Doubleday)**

MURDER IN COWETA COUNTY by Margaret Anne Barnes (Reader's Digest Press)

THE MICHIGAN MURDERS by Edward Keyes (Reader's Digest Press)

1976

A TIME TO DIE **by Tom Wicker (Quadrangle NY Times)**

THE HOUSE ON GARIBALDI STREET by Isser Harel (Viking)

INVITATION TO A LYNCHING by Gene Miller (Doubleday)

1975

HELTER SKELTER **by Vincent Bugliosi and Curt Gentry (Norton)**

THE MEMPHIS MURDERS by Gerald Meyer (Seabury Press)

DUMMY by Ernest Tidyman (Little, Brown)

1974

LEGACY OF DEATH **by Barbara Levy (Prentice-Hall)**

BURDEN OF PROOF by Ed Cray (Macmillan)

THE MEDICAL DETECTIVES by Paulette Cooper (David McKay)

THE IMPLOSION OF CONSPIRACY by Louis Nizer (Doubleday)

THE PROFESSION OF VIOLENCE by John Pearson (Saturday Review Press)

1973

HOAX by Stephen Fay, Lewis Chester and Magnus Linkletter (Viking)

THE SANTA CLAUS BANK ROBBERY by A. C. Greene (Knopf)

THEY GOT TO FIND ME GUILTY YET by T. P. Slattery (Doubleday)

SHIPWRECK by Gordon Thomas and Max Morgan Witts (Stein & Day)

1972

BEYOND A REASONABLE DOUBT by Sandor Frankel (Stein & Day)

THE GIRL ON THE VOLKSWAGEN FLOOR by William A. Clark (Harper & Row)

THE DISAPPEARANCE OF DR. PARKMAN by Robert Sullivan (Little, Brown)

1971

A GREAT FALL by Mildred Savage (Simon & Schuster)

THE NINTH JUROR by Girard Chester (Random House)

CRIME IN AMERICA by Ramsey Clark (Simon & Schuster)

1970

THE CASE THAT WILL NOT DIE by Herbert Ehrmann (Little, Brown)

SCOTTSBORO by Don T. Carter (Lousiana State University Press)

THE VICTIMS by Bernard Lefkowitz and Kenneth Gross (Putnam)

WHITMORE by Fred C. Shapiro (Bobbs-Merrill)

1969

POE THE DETECTIVE by John Walsh (Rutgers University Press)

THE MULBERRY TREE by John Frasca (Prentice-Hall)

THREE SISTERS IN BLACK by Norman Zierold (Little, Brown)

1968

A PRIVATE DISGRACE by Victoria Lincoln (Putnam)

FRAME-UP by Curt Gentry (Norton)

BLACK MARKET MEDICINE by Margaret Kreig (Prentice-Hall)

JUSTICE IN THE BACK ROOM by Selwyn Raab (World Publishing Co.)

1967

THE BOSTON STRANGLER by Gerold Frank (NAL)

THE LAST TWO TO HANG by Elwyn Jones (Stein & Day)

CRIME AND DETECTION by Julian Symons (Crown)

1966

IN COLD BLOOD by Truman Capote (Random House)

MURDERERS SANE AND MAD by Miriam Allen deFord (Abelard-Schuman)

THE POWER OF LIFE AND DEATH by Michael V. DiSalle with Lawrence G. Blochman (Random House)

A LITTLE GIRL IS DEAD by Harry Golden (World)

THE CENTURY OF THE DETECTIVE by Jurgen Thorwald (Harcourt, Brace & World)

1965

GIDEON'S TRUMPET by Anthony Lewis (Random House)

THE MOLLY MAGUIRES by Wayne G. Broehl, Jr. (Harvard University Press)

THE MINISTER AND THE CHOIR SINGER by William Kunstler (Wm. Morrow)

LAMENT FOR THE MOLLY MAGUIRES by Arthur H. Lewis (Harcourt, Brace & World)

THE HONORED SOCIETY by Norman Lewis (Putnam)

1964

THE DEED by Gerold Frank (Simon & Schuster)

FLIGHT 967 by Brad Williams (Wm. Morrow)

THE HIRED KILLERS by Peter Wyden (Wm. Morrow)

1963

TRAGEDY IN DEDHAM by Francis Russell (McGraw-Hill)

1962

DEATH AND THE SUPREME COURT **by Barrett Prettyman, Jr. (Harcourt, Brace & World)**

THE SHEPPARD MURDER CASE by Paul Holmes (McKay)

LIZZIE BORDEN: THE UNTOLD STORY by Edward D. Radin (Simon & Schuster)

KIDNAP by George Waller (Dial)

1961

THE OVERBURY AFFAIR **by Miriam Allen deFord (Chilton)**

HEAVEN KNOWS WHO by Christianna Brand (Scribner's)

MOSTLY MURDER by Sir Sydney Smith (McKay)

1960

FIRE AT SEA **by Thomas Gallager (Rinehart)**

GREAT TRAIN ROBBERIES OF THE WEST by Eugene B. Block (Coward-McCann)

1959

THEY DIED IN THE CHAIR **by Wenzell Brown (Popular Library)**

THE ROYAL VULTURES by Sam Kollman as told to Hillel Black (Pocket Books)

THE MURDER AND THE TRIAL by Edgar Lustgarten (Scribner's)

THE DEADLY REASONS by Edward D. Radin (Popular Library)

THE INCURABLE WOUND by Berton Roueche (Little, Brown)

1958

THE D.A.'S MAN **by Harold R. Danforth and James D. Horan (Crown)**

MEMOIRS OF A BOW STREET RUNNER by Henry Goddard, edited by Patrick Pringle (Wm. Morrow)

THE GIRL IN THE BELFRY by Lenore Glen Offord and Joseph Henry Jackson (Gold Medal)

1957

NIGHT FELL ON GEORGIA **by Charles and Louise Samuels (Dell)**

RUBY MCCOLLUM, THE WOMAN IN THE SUWANNE JAIL by William Bradford Huie (Dutton)

HISTORICAL WHODUNITS by Hugh Ross Williamson (Macmillan)

1956

DEAD AND GONE **by Manly Wade Wellman (University of North Carolina Press)**

THE TRUTH ABOUT BELLE GUNNESS by Lillian de la Torre (Gold Medal)

THE ASSASSINS by Robert J. Donovan (Harper)

1955

THE GIRL WITH THE SCARLET BRAND **by Charles Boswell and Lewis Thompson**

1954

WHY DID THEY KILL? **by John Bartlow Martin (Ballantine)**

1953

COURT OF LAST RESORT **by Erle Stanley Gardner (Wm. Sloane Assoc.)**

1952

TRUE TALES FROM THE ANNALS OF CRIME AND RASCALITY **by St. Clair McKelway**

LADY KILLERS by W. T. Brannon

1951

TWELVE AGAINST CRIME **by Edward D. Radin (Putnam)**

William T. Brannon for general excellence in fact crime writing

1950

BAD COMPANY **by Joseph Henry Jackson (Harcourt, Brace & World)**

1949

Marie Rodell for her editorship of the *REGIONAL MURDER* series (Duell, Sloan & Pearce)

1948

TWELVE AGAINST THE LAW by **Edward D. Radin (Duell, Sloan and Pearce)**

Best Critical/Biographical Work · (NEW CATEGORY AS OF 1977)

1994

THE SAINT: A COMPLETE HISTORY by **Burl Barer (McFarland & Co.)**

THE FINE ART OF MURDER edited by Ed Gorman, Martin H. Greenberg, Larry Segriff, with Jon L. Breen (Carroll & Graf)

A READER'S GUIDE TO THE AMERICAN NOVEL OF DETECTION by Marvin Lachman (G. K. Hall)

THE MAN WHO WASN'T MAIGRET by Patrick Marnham (Farrar, Straus & Giroux)

DOROTHY L. SAYERS: HER LIFE AND SOUL by Barbara Reynolds (St. Martin's)

1993

ALIAS S. S. VAN DINE by **John Loughery (Scribner's)**

DOROTHY L. SAYERS: A CARELESS RAGE FOR LIFE by David Coomes (Lion Publishing)

EDGAR ALLAN POE: HIS LIFE AND LEGACY by Jeffrey Meyers (Scribner's)

DOUBLEDAY CRIME CLUB COMPENDIUM, 1928–1991 by Ellen Nehr (Offspring Press)

1992

EDGAR A. POE: MOURNFUL AND NEVER-ENDING REMEMBRANCE by Kenneth Silverman (HarperCollins)

OUT OF THE WOODPILE: BLACK CHARACTERS IN CRIME AND DETECTIVE FICTION by Frankie E. Bailey (Greenwood Press)

AGATHA CHRISTIE: MURDER IN FOUR ACTS by Peter Haining (Virgin Books)

TALKING MYSTERIES: A CONVERSATION WITH TONY HILLERMAN by Tony Hillerman and Ernie Bulow (University of New Mexico Press)

JIM THOMPSON: SLEEP WITH THE DEVIL by Michael J. McCauley (Mysterious Press)

1991

TROUBLE IS THEIR BUSINESS: PRIVATE EYES IN FICTION, FILM, AND TELEVISION, 1927–1988 by John Conquest (Garland)

JOHN DICKSON CARR: A CRITICAL STUDY by S. T. Joshi (Bowling Green Popular Press)

THE REMARKABLE CASE OF DOROTHY L. SAYERS by Catherine Kenney (Kent State University Press)

ERIC AMBLER by Peter Lewis (Continuum)

HILLARY WAUGH'S GUIDE TO MYSTERIES AND MYSTERY WRITING by Hillary Waugh (Writer's Digest Books)

1990

THE LIFE OF GRAHAM GREENE, VOLUME 1: 1904–1939 by Norman Sherry (Viking)

FILM NOIR: REFLECTIONS IN A DARK MIRROR by Bruce Crowther (Continuum)

MYSTERIUM AND MYSTERY: THE CLERICAL CRIME NOVEL by William David Spencer (UMI Research Press)

THE PERFECT MURDER: A STUDY IN DETECTION by David Lehman (Free Press/Macmillan)

MURDER ON THE AIR by Ric Meyers (Mysterious Press)

1989

CORNELL WOOLRICH: FIRST YOU DREAM, THEN YOU DIE by **Francis M. Nevins, Jr. (Mysterious Press)**

THE DIME DETECTIVES by Ron Goulart (Mysterious Press)

SILK STALKINGS: WHEN WOMEN WRITE OF MURDER by Victoria Nichols and Susan Thompson (Black Lizard)

SISTERS IN CRIME: FEMINISM AND THE CRIME NOVEL by Maureen T. Reddy (Continuum)

1988

INTRODUCTION TO THE DETECTIVE STORY by **Leroy Lad Panek (Popular Press)**

CRIME & MYSTERY, THE 100 BEST BOOKS by H. R. F. Keating (Carroll & Graf)

CAMPION'S CAREER: A STUDY OF THE NOVELS OF MARGERY ALLINGHAM by B. A. Pike (Bowling Green Popular Press)

CORRIDORS OF DECEIT, THE WORLD OF JOHN LE CARRÉ by Peter Wolfe (Popular Library)

1987

HERE LIES: AN AUTOBIOGRAPHY by **Eric Ambler (Farrar, Straus & Giroux)**

THE SECRET OF THE STRATEMEYER SYNDICATE: NANCY DREW, THE HARDY BOYS & THE MILLION DOLLAR FICTION FACTORY by Carol Billman (Ungar)

THE MYSTERY LOVER'S COMPANION by Art Bourgeau (Crown)

13 MISTRESSES OF MURDER by Elaine Budd (Ungar)

1001 MIDNIGHTS: THE AFICIONADO'S GUIDE TO MYSTERY FICTION by Bill Pronzini and Marcia Muller (Arbor House)

1986

JOHN LE CARRÉ by **Peter Lewis (Ungar)**

PRIVATE EYES: 101 KNIGHTS, A SURVEY OF AMERICAN FICTION by Robert A. Baker and Michael T. Nietzel (Bowling Green Popular Press)

THE LORD PETER WIMSEY COMPANION by Stephan P. Clarke (Mysterious Press)

THE AMERICAN PRIVATE EYE: THE IMAGE IN FICTION by David Geherin (Ungar)

AGATHA CHRISTIE by Janet Morgan (Knopf)

1985

NOVEL VERDICTS: A GUIDE TO COURTROOM FICTION **by Jon L. Breen (Scarecrow Press)**

THE JAMES BOND BEDSIDE COMPANION by Raymond Benson (Dodd, Mead)

ROSS MACDONALD by Matthew J. Bruccoli (Harcourt Brace Jovanovich)

ONE LONELY KNIGHT: MICKEY SPILLANE'S MIKE HAMMER by Max Allan Collins and James L. Traylor (Bowling Green Popular Press)

INWARD JOURNEY: ROSS MACDONALD Ralph B. Sipper, editor (Cordelia Editions)

1984

THE DARK SIDE OF GENIUS: THE LIFE OF ALFRED HITCHCOCK **by Donald Spoto (Little, Brown)**

THE MYSTERY OF GEORGES SIMENON by Fenton Bresler (Beaufort)

DASHIELL HAMMETT by Diane Johnson (Random House)

THE POETICS OF MURDER Glenn W. Most and William W. Stowe, editors (Harcourt Brace Jovanovich)

1983

CAIN **by Roy Hoopes (Holt, Rinehart & Winston)**

THE POLICE PROCEDURAL by George N. Dove (Bowling Green Popular Press)

GUN IN CHEEK by Bill Pronzini (Coward, McCann & Geoghegan)

MODUS OPERANDI by Robin W. Winks (David R. Godine)

1982

WHAT ABOUT MURDER? **by Jon L. Breen (Scarecrow Press)**

THE WHODUNIT by Stefano Benvenuti and Gianni Rizzoni (Macmillan)

SELECTED LETTERS OF RAYMOND CHANDLER Frank MacShane, editor (Columbia University Press)

TV DETECTIVES by Richard Meyers (A. S. Barnes & Co.)

THE ANNOTATED TALES OF EDGAR ALLAN POE Stephen Peithman, editor (Doubleday)

1981

TWENTIETH CENTURY CRIME AND MYSTERY WRITERS by John Reilly (St. Martin's)

A TALENT TO DECEIVE: AN APPRECIATION OF AGATHA CHRISTIE by Robert Barnard (Dodd, Mead)

WATTEAU'S SHEPHERDS: THE DETECTIVE NOVEL IN BRITAIN 1914–1940 by Leroy Lad Panek (Bowling Green Popular Press)

1980

DOROTHY L. SAYERS, A LITERARY BIOGRAPHY by Ralph E. Hone (Kent State University Press)

THE SECRETS OF GROWN-UPS by Vera Caspary (McGraw-Hill)

AS HER WHIMSEY TOOK HER Margaret Hannay, editor (Kent State University Press)

SHERLOCK HOLMES, THE MAN AND HIS WORLD by H. R. F. Keating (Scribner's)

1979

THE MYSTERY OF AGATHA CHRISTIE by Gwen Robins (Doubleday)

ERLE STANLEY GARDNER: THE CASE OF THE REAL PERRY MASON by Dorothy B. Hughes (Wm. Morrow)

THE TELL-TALE HEART: THE LIFE AND WORK OF EDGAR ALLAN POE by Julian Symons (Harper & Row)

THE DETECTIVE IN HOLLYWOOD by John Tuska (Doubleday)

1978

REX STOUT by John McAleer (Little, Brown)

AN AUTOBIOGRAPHY by Agatha Christie (Dodd, Mead)

THE ENCYCLOPEDIA SHERLOCKIANA by Jack Tracy (Doubleday)

1977

ENCYCLOPEDIA OF MYSTERY AND DETECTION by Chris Steinbrunner, Otto Penzler, Marvin Lachman and Charles Shibuk (McGraw-Hill)

THE MYSTERY STORY John Ball, editor (University of California at San Diego Publishers)

THE DANGEROUS EDGE by Gavin Lambert (Grossman)

THE LIFE OF RAYMOND CHANDLER by Frank McShane (Dutton)

THE AGATHA CHRISTIE MYSTERY by Derrick Murdoch (Pagurian Press)

List of Contributors

GARY ALEXANDER
Blood Sacrifice
Doubleday

CHRISTINE ANDREAE
Trail of Murder
St. Martin's

SARAH ANDREWS
Tensleep
Otto Penzler Books

BARBARA ANDREWS
(PAMELA ROCK)
Moon of Desire
Leisure Books

CHARLES ARDAI
Kingpins
Carroll & Graf

MIGNON F. BALLARD
Minerva Cries Murder
Carroll & Graf

RAYMOND E. BANKS
Computer Kill
Popular Publications

CAROL BARKIN
(BEVERLY HASTINGS)
Somebody Help Me
Berkley

LINDA BARNES
Snapshot
Delacorte

LARRY BEINHART
American Hero
Pantheon/Ballantine

RAYMOND BENSON
The James Bond Bedside Companion
Boxtree, Ltd.

LAURIEN BERENSON
Night Cries
Harper Paperbacks

PETER BLAUNER
Casino Moon
Simon & Schuster

JOHN C. BOLAND
Rich Man's Blood
St. Martin's

J. S. BORTHWICK
Dude on Arrival
St. Martin's

JAY BRANDON
Rules of Evidence
Pocket Books

JON L. BREEN
Hot Air
Simon & Schuster

BETTY BUCHANAN
Tender Is the Knife
David McKay

CAROL BUDD
Scarlet Scandals
Pocket Books

CAROL CAIL
Private Lies
Harper Paperbacks

GEORGE C. CHESBRO
An Incident at Bloodtide
Mysterious Press

JOYCE CHRISTMAS
It's Her Funeral
Ballantine/Fawcett

RICHARD CICIARELLI
short stories

STEPHAN P. CLARKE
*The Lord Peter Wimsey
Companion*
Mysterious Press

EDWARD CLINE
We Three Kings
The Atlantean Press

ANDREW COBURN
No Way Home
Dutton

STANLEY COHEN
Angel Face
St. Martin's

MAX ALLAN COLLINS
Murder by the Numbers
St. Martin's

ANNA ASHWOOD COLLINS
Red Roses for a Dead Trucker
Kodansha

MICHAEL COLLINS
Cassandra in Red
Donald I. Fine

SUSAN CONANT
Bloodlines
Doubleday

PETRONELLE COOK
(MARGOT ARNOLD)
The Cape Cod Conundrum
Foul Play Press

MICHAEL CORMANY
Skin Deep Is Fatal
Heldman/Birch Lane Press

PHILIP R. CRAIG
The Double Minded Men
Scribner's

DAN CRAWFORD
Rouse a Sleeping Cat
Ace

BILL CRIDER
Booked for a Hanging
St. Martin's

ANN CROWLEIGH
(BARBARA CUMMINGS
& JO-ANN POWER)
Dead As Dead Can Be
Zebra

BARBARA D'AMATO
Hard Women
Scribner's

BRIAN D'AMATO
Beauty
Delacorte

ALZINA STONE DALE
*Mystery Readers' Walk Guide:
London*
Passport Books

SANDY DANGLER
Death Valley
Moody Press

DOROTHY B. DAVIS
short stories

DOROTHY SALISBURY DAVIS
The Habit of Fear
Scribner's

J. MADISON DAVIS
Red Knight
Walker

JIM DEFILIPPI
Blood Sugar
HarperCollins

ROBERT DICHIARA
The Dick and the Devil
Tor Books

CAROLE NELSON DOUGLAS
Catnap
St. Martin's/Tor

JAMES T. DOYLE
Epitaph for a Loser
Walker

LOIS DU LAC
short stories

BRENDAN DUBOIS
Dead Sand
Otto Penzler Books

DONALD A. DURKEE
(RICHARD BLAINE)
The Tainted Jade
Pageant

AARON ELKINS
Old Scores
Scribner's

P. N. ELROD
Blood on the Water
Ace

KATHY LYNN EMERSON
Echoes and Illusions
Harper Paperbacks

STEVE ENGLEHART
The Point Man
Dell

TERRY FAIN
short stories

ANN C. FALLON
Dead Ends
Pocket Books